Visits to Heaven and Back—Are They Real?

Visits to Heaven and Back
ARE THEY REAL?

Mark Hitchcock

Tyndale House Publishers, Inc.
Carol Stream, Illinois

Library of Congress Cataloging-in-Publication Data
Hitchcock, Mark, date.
 Visits to heaven and back, are they real? / Mark Hitchcock.
  pages cm
 Includes bibliographical references.
 ISBN 978-1-4964-0482-4 (sc)
 1. Near-death experiences—Religious aspects—Christianity. 2. Heaven—Christianity.
I. Title.
 BT833.H58 2015
 236'.24—dc23   2014044541

Printed in the United States of America

21 20 19 18 17 16 15
 7   6   5   4   3   2   1

To my grandson, Gavin Gray Hitchcock
I can't believe the joy you've already brought to my life
in such a brief time. I pray for you every day. May the
Lord grant us many years to enjoy here on earth and the
blessing of eternity together in our heavenly home.

Contents

There are three heavens.

The first heaven is where the birds fly;

the second heaven is where the stars are;

and the third heaven is the abode of God.

The first heaven we see by day;

the second heaven we see by night;

and the third heaven we see by faith.

ADRIAN ROGERS

I want to know one thing, the way to heaven; how to land safe on that happy shore. God Himself has condescended to teach the way; for this end He came from heaven. He hath written it down in a book. Give me that book! At any price give me the Book of God!

JOHN WESLEY

CHAPTER 1

HEAVEN CAN'T WAIT

Dear God,

What is it like when a person dies? Nobody will tell me. I just want to
*   know, I don't want to do it.*

Your friend,

Mike

VISITS TO HEAVEN and back are where it's at today. Some of the runaway bestsellers in the last few years are tales of heavenly tourism. Interest in near-death experiences (NDEs) has exploded. The fascination over what happens after death has reached critical mass. Heaven is hot. In just the last decade, dozens of heavenly memoirs have piled into bookstores and online retailers. They fill and even top the bestseller lists. Book sales for this new genre are stratospheric.

The stories of heaven come from people of every age and all walks of life: young children, teenagers, mothers, fathers, grandmothers, pastors, orthopedists, neurosurgeons—the list goes on and on. Most of these stories are born out of terrible tragedies—horrific car accidents, drowning, electrocution, grave illness, or serious surgery. The stories of life-and-death struggles in these books are captivating by themselves. Each story is unique and filled with page-turning details. They pack a powerful emotional punch. They tug strongly on the heartstrings. But adding the dimension of traveling to heaven and back puts them over the top—literally. The craving for these books is insatiable. The world in general, and Christians in particular, seem to be obsessed with travels to heaven and back.

Why the soaring success? Clearly these books have tapped into the universal human longing to peer behind the veil of death to get a sneak preview of the afterlife. As Douglas Jacoby says, "The afterlife is a subject that interests everyone, because it is about the one thing that happens to us all. Ultimately, nothing could be more relevant."[1] He's right. What happens after death is a timeless topic. Dealing with death is not optional. Everyone wants to know what happens after we exhale our last breath.

C. S. Lewis, in "The Weight of Glory," wrote poignantly of "the inconsolable secret" that resides in each of us. He spoke of how all of us "remain conscious of a desire which no natural happiness will satisfy." Lewis said that we possess a "longing to be acknowledged, to meet with some response, to bridge some chasm that yawns between us and reality . . . to be reunited with something in the universe from which we now feel cut off, to be on the inside of some door which we have always seen from the outside." We yearn, he says, for a "welcome into the heart of things."[2] What could meet this universal need and be marketed with greater success than heavenly stories that make us feel like we know what life after death holds for us—stories that speak intimately of God, Jesus, angels, and departed loved ones and a glorious destiny that awaits us all?

People everywhere are searching for a preview, a sneak peek behind the curtain to get a jump on the afterlife. The yearning to know just a little more, the urge for any insight, no matter how trivial, is irrepressible. Fresh stories about visits to heaven and back hold out the hope that our longing to know more can be satisfied. For many who have gone through tragedy themselves or who have lost a dear friend or loved one, these books are consulted for comfort, hope, and reassurance about life after death. Grieving hearts grasping for meaning and answers are particularly drawn to these stories. After all, there's a yearning to believe that our deceased friends or loved ones are happy and satisfied in the hereafter.

The Third Wave

Stories about visits to heaven and back are a fairly recent phenomenon. The brief history of this sensation can be captured in three waves. The first wave of interest in afterlife experiences hit in the 1970s when reports of NDEs were first publicized. Raymond Moody's *Life After Life*, published in 1975, investigated the experiences of more than one hundred people who were clinically dead but then resuscitated.

Moody discovered that virtually all of his subjects shared a common, positive, enlightening experience during their near-death condition. Moody's second book, *Reflections on Life After Life* (1977), drew on more NDEs and discovered more common, recurring elements in these experiences. The world was hooked. People have been gripped with back-from-the-dead stories of NDEs ever since. Pandora's box has been opened.

In the 1990s, the second wave rolled in with the accounts of Betty Eadie (*Embraced by the Light*, 1992) and Dannion Brinkley (*Saved by the Light*, 1994). These books hit the *New York Times* Best Sellers List. Both of them contain mystical, New Age, and ultimately unbiblical teachings. (We'll talk about Betty Eadie's book in more detail in chapter 3.) Writing in the mid-1990s about the second wave of heaven-and-back books, Tal Brooke said, "What is different about the second wave is that the public seems ready to accept these reports at face value. And this includes a large cross section of Christians who have broken rank, crossing over into the realm of the occult without even knowing it."[3]

The third wave, perhaps better characterized as a tsunami, hit in 2004 with *90 Minutes in Heaven* by Don Piper. From that time until today, we've witnessed an explosion of firsthand accounts from people who claim to have visited heaven and from a few who claim to have made the round-trip to hell and back. Judging by the sales numbers, the endorsements of well-known pastors, and the positive word-of-mouth these books have generated, the public has embraced and celebrated these memoirs, accepting one after another with open hearts and minds. Their mushrooming popularity has resulted in hundreds of books on this topic, many of them bestsellers with a few selling millions of copies. *Heaven Is for Real*—the gold standard for heaven-and-back stories—has sold almost ten million copies, and at the time I'm writing these words, it still sits near the top one hundred books on Amazon. Sony Pictures released a movie version of *Heaven Is for Real* in spring 2014, and it earned over $100 million in the worldwide box office.[4]

I expect these to-heaven-and-back books to continue to roll off the presses because the popularity and staggering sales numbers are hard to ignore. As Craig Wilson says, "Just ask any bookseller in America. Folks have been going to heaven with amazing regularity lately. . . . It's a lucrative journey. Three of these tales have ascended to heavenly heights on USA Today's best-seller list recently, and more are on the way."[5]

So you can get a feel for just how big this phenomenon is, here's a brief list, in alphabetical order, of forty of the main books in this burgeoning genre:

- Eben Alexander, *Proof of Heaven: A Neurosurgeon's Journey into the Afterlife*
- Reggie Anderson, *Appointments with Heaven: The True Story of a Country Doctor's Healing Encounters with the Hereafter*

- P. M. H. Atwater and David H. Morgan, *The Complete Idiot's Guide to Near-Death Experiences*
- Mary Baxter, *A Divine Revelation of Heaven*
- Mary Baxter, *A Divine Revelation of Hell*
- Marvin J. Besteman, *My Journey to Heaven: What I Saw and How It Changed My Life*
- Dale Black, *Flight to Heaven: A Plane Crash . . . A Lone Survivor . . . A Journey to Heaven—and Back*
- Dannion Brinkley, *Saved by the Light*
- Ben Brocard, *I Went to Heaven and I Saw God*
- Richard Bullivant, *Heaven and the Afterlife: Is Heaven Real? True Life Stories from Those Who Died and Live to Tell the Tale*
- Todd Burpo, *Heaven Is for Real: A Little Boy's Astounding Story of His Trip to Heaven and Back*
- Patrick Doucette, *Is Heaven for Real?: Personal Stories of Visiting Heaven*
- Jesse Duplantis, *Heaven: Close Encounters of the God Kind*
- James L. Garlow and Keith Wall, *Encountering Heaven and the Afterlife: True Stories from People Who Have Glimpsed the World Beyond*
- Celeste and Matthew Goodwin, *A Boy Back from Heaven*
- Trudy Harris, *Glimpses of Heaven: True Stories of Hope and Peace at the End of Life's Journey* (This book was released in 2008 and was still on the *New York Times* Best Sellers List in August 2014.)

- Trudy Harris, *More Glimpses of Heaven: Inspiring True Stories of Hope and Peace at the End of Life's Journey*
- Lonnie Honeycutt, *Death, Heaven and Back: The True Story of One Man's Death and Resurrection*
- Kat Kerr, Walter Reynolds, and Scribe Angels, *Revealing Heaven: An Eyewitness Account*
- Roberts Liardon, *Life After Death: What I Saw in Heaven*
- Roberts Liardon, *We Saw Heaven: True Stories of What Awaits You on the Other Side*
- Kevin and Alex Malarkey, *The Boy Who Came Back from Heaven: A Remarkable Account of Miracles, Angels, and Life beyond This World*
- Crystal McVea and Alex Tresniowski, *Waking Up in Heaven: A True Story of Brokenness, Heaven, and Life Again*
- Elisa Medhus, *My Son and the Afterlife: Conversations from the Other Side*
- Grady Mosby, *A Near Death Experience: I Died and Came Back from Hell*
- Mary C. Neal, *To Heaven and Back: A Doctor's Extraordinary Account of Her Death, Heaven, Angels, and Life Again: A True Story*
- Don Piper, *90 Minutes in Heaven: A True Story of Death and Life*
- John Pontius, *Visions of Glory: One Man's Astonishing Account of the Last Days*
- John W. Price, *Revealing Heaven: The Eyewitness*

*Accounts That Changed How a Pastor Thinks about the
Afterlife*
- Dennis and Nolene Prince, *Nine Days in Heaven: The
Vision of Marietta Davis*
- Tessy Rawlins, *Near Death Experiences; True Stories of
Those Who Went to Heaven*
- Sid Roth and Lonnie Lane, *Heaven Is beyond Your
Wildest Expectations: Ten True Stories of Experiencing
Heaven*
- Vassula Ryden, *Heaven Is Real but So Is Hell: An
Eyewitness Account of What Is to Come*
- Jenny Sharkey and Ian McCormack, *Clinically Dead:
I've Seen Heaven and Hell*
- Richard Sigmund, *My Time in Heaven: A True Story of
Dying and Coming Back*
- Howard Storm, *My Descent into Death: A Second
Chance at Life*
- David E. Taylor, *My Trip to Heaven: Face to Face with
Jesus*
- Heidi Telpner, *One Foot in Heaven: Journey of a
Hospice Nurse*
- Freddy Vest, *The Day I Died: My Astonishing Trip to
Heaven and Back*
- Bill Wiese, *23 Minutes in Hell: One Man's Story about
What He Saw, Heard, and Felt in That Place of Torment*

The list could go on and on and probably will. The addiction to heavenly travelogues shows no signs of abating.

Fact, Fantasy, or Fraud?

The commercial success of these books is undeniable. Still, there is some cause for concern with these heavenly memoirs. My worry is that people want the message of these books to be true so badly that they are willing to consume these stories and instinctively believe them, often with little or no discernment. The language is sensational, fascinating, and appealing, and people everywhere believe it.[6] But should we? That's the key question I want to address in this book. What are we to make of these stories? Are they fact, fantasy, or fraud?

My interest in answering this question was aroused during a fascinating conversation at 30,000 feet. My wife and I were on a Southwest Airlines flight from our home in Oklahoma City to a speaking engagement in California. I was reading *Heaven Is for Real* on the plane. The movie version of the book was about to debut, and I had watched an interview on one of the network morning shows with the authors, Todd and Colton Burpo. My interest was piqued. I wanted to find out whether the runaway bestseller was as great as some people had told me or whether it was garbage as others had reported—or somewhere in between. I had my suspicions, but the only way to find out for sure was to read the book for myself.

The woman next to me saw that I was reading the book and told me she liked it very much. She was the librarian at a Baptist church in Texas. "How do you like it?" she asked me.

By that time I was about three-fourths of the way through.

I told her that the story of Colton's medical issues and recovery was encouraging but that I didn't put any stock in the account of his trip to heaven and back. Somewhat surprised, she asked me why I felt that way. Not knowing her or how she might respond, I carefully and thoughtfully (I hope) outlined some of the specific statements in the book that I believe contradict Scripture (which I'll look at in detail in chapter 6).

She listened to what I had to say and then said, "You know, I've never considered some of those things." But then she added, "Well, at least the book will do a lot of good by getting people to think about heaven and life after death."

"God can certainly use books like *Heaven Is for Real* for his purposes," I responded, "and it can spur beneficial conversations about heaven and life after death, but heaven-and-back books can also do a great deal of damage by giving people a wrong view of heaven or failing to accurately tell them how to get there." I added, "Or in some cases these books can actually lull readers into the false belief that everyone goes to heaven."

She graciously nodded and seemed to agree with what I had said. She thanked me and said, "You've given me a lot to think about."

As I reflected on our conversation, the idea for this book crystallized. I thought about the millions of people like the woman on the airplane who had never thought about the ramifications of heavenly memoirs that are not scripturally sound. I thought about that woman's comments and how we all have to be careful not to adopt the pragmatic argument that just because God can bring good out of bad, the bad is acceptable or not really that bad. Of course, God is sovereign, but that's no excuse for promoting error. Professing Christians who write books—even books about very personal experiences—are responsible to make every effort to interpret Scripture accurately and at least not to directly contradict it.

I realize many people today instantly recoil when anyone questions books they view as innocent, and which have purportedly helped bring hope and encouragement to so many people. Some might say, "Aren't these books just harmless speculation? What's the big deal? Why pick on these books that seem to be giving so many people comfort and hope? Who are you to question someone else's experience?" I understand that attitude. The prevailing notion today is that it's unloving and uncharitable to question someone else's experience or private revelation from God. So I realize at the outset that some, maybe even many, will dismiss or even reject any appraisal or critique of these books out of hand. Of course, that's their choice, but we are all subject to God's Word. I have nothing personal against any of the people who have written about trips to heaven and back. I'm sure most of them are very nice, sincere people. But with the astonishing popularity of these books, I'm sure there will be many more to come. Thus, it's incumbent on believers to discern the truth of the claims being made and to think biblically about heaven and the afterlife.

One overriding message in most of these books is that there is nothing to fear in the afterlife. They are full of unconditional love no matter who you are, what you've done, or what you haven't done. That's part of the attraction of these books in our modern culture, where tolerance and acceptance are worshiped. The message of these books meshes with how people want heaven to be. But we have to ask—is that how heaven is presented in God's Word? In the pages that follow, I want to answer that question and many more:

- What are we to make of this publishing phenomenon?
- Can we dismiss these books as harmless speculation?
- Are NDEs real?
- Are people really going to heaven (and in some cases hell) and coming back?
- Have these people met Jesus and talked with him?
- Are their descriptions reliable?
- What does the Bible say?

Heavenly Minded

Thinking about heaven, hell, and life after death, while not always practiced today, is very important to daily life. I'm all for being heavenly minded and maintaining an eternal perspective, as Scripture teaches (see Colossians 3:1-4). But as with any other area of biblical truth or theology, we have to make sure that our thinking about heaven is in line with God's Word and not the product of imagination, fantasy, or delusion. As Douglas Jacoby says, "The public appetite for the transcendent is enormous, but people need truth, not speculation."[7] I agree. There's far too much speculation and sensationalism out there today, especially concerning life after death. In this book I hope to balance this speculation and sensationalism with our only reliable source about the afterlife—Scripture. God's Word is *the* travel brochure that tells us what heaven is like and *the* road map—the navigational system—to direct us how to get there.

But before we launch into our assessment of heavenly memoirs, let's make a brief stop at the beginning point for the modern obsession with life after death—events commonly known as near-death experiences. Let's consider whether they really happen and whether they can tell us anything about eternity.

CHAPTER 2

THE ABCs OF NDEs

I'm not afraid of death, I just don't want to be there when it happens.
WOODY ALLEN

A PASSENGER IN a taxi leaned to ask the driver a question and tapped him on the shoulder. The driver screamed, lost control of the cab, nearly hit a bus, drove over the curb, and stopped inches from a large plate-glass window.

For a few moments everything was silent, and the still-shaking driver said, "I'm sorry, but you scared the daylights out of me!"

The frightened passenger apologized and said he didn't realize a mere tap on the shoulder could frighten him so much.

The driver replied, "No, no, I'm sorry. It's entirely my fault. Today is my first day driving a cab. I've been driving a hearse for the last twenty-five years."

People in our world today are jumpy. We live in uncertain, troubled times. We're jumpy and frightened about many things—not the least of which is death. No one wants death to tap them on the shoulder. Death is the final specter that haunts humanity, and its influence seems to be everywhere. We know more than our ancestors did about the diseases, dangers, and disasters that can kill us. Frightening news is plastered all over the television screen and strewn across the Internet. Death is more real, "in your face," and scary than ever before.

There's the old saying that only two things are certain in life: death and taxes. But as Randy Alcorn has pointed out, that's only half true. "There are tax evaders, but there are no death evaders."[1] So how do we cope? Obviously, people devise all kinds of coping mechanisms, but I believe for a growing number of people today, fear of the unknown is diminished and even discarded by reading stories about people who have been near death and have seen and experienced the afterlife. In uncertain times, people search for comfort. The heaven-and-back books provide this comfort and make sense out of death and eternity for many people.

Although the numbers are steadily dropping, the vast majority of Americans still believe in God, heaven, and life after death. Here are the results of a 2013 Harris poll:

- 74 percent of Americans believe in God
- 64 percent believe in life after death
- 68 percent believe in the existence of heaven

- 58 percent believe in hell and the devil
- 24 percent believe in reincarnation (that they were once another person)[2]

Added to these statistics are estimates that somewhere between 10 and 50 percent of all people in a near-death situation have some kind of experience.[3] Some studies put the number as high as 60 percent. Of course, looking at this from the other side, that means at least half of those who came close to death did not recall a near-death experience (NDE). No one knows why some have an experience near-death and others don't. Nevertheless, the emphasis in our media seems to always be on the people who *do* have an NDE, not the ones who don't. Whatever the reason, the reporting of NDEs is definitely on the rise. Dr. Eben Alexander, author of the bestseller *Proof of Heaven*, gives one medical reason for the spike in NDEs in recent years:

> In the 1960s, new techniques were developed that allowed doctors to resuscitate patients who had suffered a cardiac arrest. Patients who in former times simply would have died were now pulled back into the land of the living. Unbeknownst to them, these physicians were, through their rescue efforts, producing a breed of trans-earthly voyagers: people who had glimpsed beyond the veil and returned to tell about it. Today they number in the millions.

Alexander continues:

> In 1975, a medical student named Raymond
> Moody published a book called *Life After Life*, in
> which he described the experience of a man named
> George Ritchie. Ritchie had "died" as a result of
> cardiac arrest as a complication of pneumonia and
> been out of his body for nine minutes. He traveled
> down a tunnel, visited heavenly and hellish regions,
> met a being of light that he identified as Jesus, and
> experienced feelings of peace and well-being that
> were so intense he had difficulty putting them into
> words. The era of the modern near-death experience
> was born.[4]

Following Moody's book, Dr. Kenneth Ring wrote
*Life at Death: A Scientific Investigation of the Near-Death
Experience* (1980). These landmark books ushered in a
new era, introducing NDEs to the mainstream of popular
culture.

While the heaven and hell experiences that are the subject
of this book sometimes differ from normal NDEs (sometimes
the experiences are in the form of visions or out-of-body
incidents and are often more detailed than typical NDEs[5]),
since most of the modern heavenly memoirs are associated
with NDEs, I believe it's important to briefly consider this
entire phenomenon.

Beyond the Body

NDEs befall people who are near what's called *clinical* (reversible) death—that is, external signs of life such as consciousness, breathing, and pulse are absent. People who experience *biological* death, which is irreversible, obviously don't return to tell us what happened, so NDEs involve only instances where people are near clinical death.[6]

The classic or composite NDE involves the sense of being "out of the body"—and people looking down at their bodies while resuscitation is attempted. Suddenly, they find they are transported to another location, often through a dark tunnel or passageway. Upon arrival, communication (often nonverbal) occurs with spirit beings or a "being of light." The being or entity is usually warm and loving and sometimes conducts an evaluation of the individuals' lives. At some point, they approach a barrier or border that cannot be crossed. Eventually, they are told they have to return to earth, but often they do not want to return because the experience is so peaceful. Nevertheless, they *do* return to earth, back in their own bodies. When they awaken, they're told that they died but, fortunately, were revived. The survivors have an overpowering desire to tell others what happened and experience transformation in the way they view life, death, and others.[7]

While not everyone who claims to have had an NDE recounts all of these features, and some extra elements may be present, these are the most frequently reported experiences. Here's a summary list of the most common NDE traits:

1. **Ineffability** (recognizing that no words can adequately explain the experience)
2. **Hearing the News** (hearing a medical professional declare them dead)
3. **Feelings of Peace and Quiet** (sensing intense pleasure and peace)
4. **The Noise** (hearing a distinct sound at or near death that can be pleasant or disturbing)
5. **The Dark Tunnel** (traveling through a passageway)
6. **Out of Body** (seeing their body apart from themselves)
7. **Meeting Others** (encountering some spiritual being—sometimes angels, Jesus, or a departed loved one—to guide them through the experience.
8. **The Being of Light** (beholding a brilliant light that emanates from a being who radiates love and who communicates by thoughts, not audible speech)
9. **The Review** (witnessing a vivid panoramic review of their life)
10. **The Border or Limit** (feeling an obstruction or barrier, often a fence, door, or body of water that keeps them from going any further in their journey)
11. **Coming Back** (returning back to their body—some wanting to stay with the being of light and others choosing to return)
12. **Telling Others** (disclosing the experience with reticence because of the skepticism of others and the inability to adequately describe what happened)

13. **Effects on Lives** (viewing life and others in a different light)
14. **New Views of Death** (losing the fear of death)
15. **Corroboration** (verifying the experience by relating details or specific incidents that happened while the person was supposedly dead—for instance, events in the hospital operating or waiting room)[8]

As we assess some of the main heaven-and-back books in the next four chapters, you'll see these details pop up again and again.

Magical Mystery Tour

As you can imagine, there are numerous theories to explain NDEs. Many of these theories are skeptical, offering a variety of natural explanations. Some of the most common causes for NDEs include the following:

- hallucinations induced by pain or medication
- leftover memories from the birth experience
- the reaction of the brain to altered levels of oxygen and carbon dioxide
- psychological wish fulfillment (hoping there is a heaven)
- a defense mechanism (mentally leaving the body and watching what's happening as a third person)
- temporal lobe seizures
- sensory deprivation[9]

While each of these explanations makes sense to some degree, from all I've read, it doesn't seem that *all* NDEs can be explained away by natural factors. The evidence to the contrary is simply too overwhelming to dismiss them all by psychological, pharmacological, or neurological explanations. Of course, many who claim to have these experiences would argue against natural factors, as do many with strong New Age and occultic leanings. But many Christians also believe natural factors are insufficient to explain *all* NDEs.

Two of the foremost Christian scholars in this area are Gary R. Habermas and J. P. Moreland. While I don't agree with all their conclusions, they do an excellent job of weighing the various issues related to NDEs. After extensive research, they believe that NDEs are "verified as objective and reliable" and that they provide proof of existence after death—that "we survive our bodies."[10] I believe that much is clear. *Something* is happening that can't be written off by purely natural causes. Habermas and Moreland maintain it's possible that some aspects of NDEs are related to occultic spiritual realities and Satanic counterfeit but reject the notion that all NDEs are occultic or unbiblical. They observe, "Just as you can't have fake money without real money, so you can't have fake NDEs without real ones. You can't counterfeit what doesn't exist."[11]

In spite of their acceptance of NDEs as real and proof of life after death, Habermas and Moreland reject their effectiveness for conveying reliable details about heaven and hell. They write, "We hold that NDEs cannot be used to describe (or interpret) details concerning heaven or hell. Interpretation regarding heaven and hell and the identity of religious persons cannot be verified (on this side of the grave, at least)."[12] This is a very important point. Despite accepting that NDEs are "verified as objective and reliable," they disregard NDEs as trustworthy guides to what heaven is like. Habermas and Moreland conclude

- NDEs are real (something is happening to many people near death).
- NDEs are proof of life after death. (I wouldn't put this point quite as strongly. I would say more cautiously that NDEs don't prove life after death but do suggest it is possible or even probable.)
- NDEs reflect the popular concepts of the afterlife reflected at the time.
- Some NDEs may be occultic and Satanic counterfeits.
- NDEs cannot be used as reliable guides to describe details about heaven or hell.

Habermas and Moreland add this caveat: "Interpretations of one's experiences are notoriously tricky things. Interpretations of even everyday episodes sometimes vary widely from person to person. This by no means indicates that things don't really happen as they appear, only that we should be very careful about reporting them and especially our opinions *about* them."[13]

Dead or Alive?

Clouding this entire issue is the essential question—when is a person really dead, and can people who are only *near* death tell us anything reliable about death? Dinesh D'Souza, whose wife allegedly had an "out of body" experience after an automobile accident, admits, "By definition no one has reported a near death experience that fully crossed that barrier from this life to the next."[14] Near death is not death. *Death* is death. No matter how close to biological death you get, if you don't die irreversibly, then you do not experience true physical death, which is the permanent separation of the human spirit from the body (see James 2:26). And true death—real death—only happens one time (see Hebrews 9:27). Therefore, if someone did not die, then how seriously should I or anyone else take that person's claims of knowing what happens *after* death? Is near death close enough?

Years ago, in *Christianity Today*, an article about NDEs made this clever comparison. The author's analogy went like this: What if you were taking a trip to Denver, Colorado, and needed directions to get there and then find a specific location in the city? Would you ask a friend who had been near Denver but had never stepped inside the city limits? Would you trust his NDE (Near-Denver Experience) as accurate and reliable? Or would you prefer to get your directions from someone who had actually been to and was familiar with Denver?[15] There's a big difference between near Denver and Denver, and an even bigger chasm between near death and death.

Jesus is the only one who has died, been to the other side, and come back to tell us about it. He is the only one who is qualified to tell us what lies behind the veil of death. Decades after his resurrection, Jesus said, "Do not be afraid; I am the first and the last, and the living One; and I was dead, and behold, I am alive forevermore, and I have the keys of death and of Hades" (Revelation 1:17-18, NASB). We would be wise to get our information about heaven and directions about how to get there from him and his Word. That's what I want us to do in this book.

Near-Death Disclaimer

Before we embark on our careful consideration of the claims in some of the main heaven-and-back books, I want to issue an important disclaimer. I won't venture in this book to explain what happened to the authors of these heavenly memoirs we'll examine. Many suggestions have been offered. Some say the alleged trips to heaven and back are demonic. Others believe they're dreams or induced by chemicals in the brain or medication, while others maintain that most of these books are motivated by greed or notoriety and that the authors are liars and frauds.

With potential sales in the millions for books of this ilk, there's always the looming danger of copycats cashing in on the popularity and excitement that's generated by these stories. I'm sure some of that has happened. We would be naive not to think so. The motivation for many of these authors may be an honest desire to help others. Theories abound. I don't profess to know what happened or what motivated the authors to write these books. No one can know the heart of someone else except God. But regardless of the motivation, I can safely and accurately say that these authors didn't go to heaven and come back. I realize that statement may sound bold. How can I be so sure? Because, as we shall see, their accounts are at odds with Scripture to varying degrees, and often even contradict one another.

The Bible is our infallible guide to life after death. Jesus is sovereign over death and the afterlife. He alone holds the keys to death and Hades (see Revelation 1:17-18). We know we can trust Jesus and what the Bible tells us about heaven because of its perfect, astounding track record of 100 percent accuracy when it comes to predicting the future. No other book even comes close. For instance, over one hundred specific prophecies were fulfilled in the life of Jesus Christ at his first coming to earth. The Bible stands alone concerning things to come.

So when accounts of visits to heaven contradict the Bible, we know that the Bible is right and the heavenly memoirs are wrong. In other cases, these books go beyond—sometimes *far* beyond—Scripture in describing various details. The implication from these accounts is that the Bible is somehow insufficient or lacking—that we need more than God has given us in his Word, in spite of God's warning not to go beyond what is written (see 1 Corinthians 4:6) or to add to his Word, including what he has told us about heaven (see

Revelation 22:18-19). The biblical information about heaven is not extensive, but it is entirely consistent. The heavenly memoirs, on the other hand, are *not* consistent with one another and are often inconsistent with the Bible, focusing at length on details and information the Bible never addresses.

The ultimate issue here is one of discernment, a trait that is desperately needed today. Even if we all agree that NDEs are real—that is, that something happens to some people near death that cannot be explained as hallucinations, wishful thinking, or simply the result of chemicals released in the brain—it doesn't necessarily follow that NDEs are reliable guides about life after death. If they are not consistent with God's Word, they must not only be doubted and discounted, they must be disregarded and denounced. Doug Groothuis pinpoints the central question: "Near-death experiences have been testified to, systematically studied by competent authorities, and certainly seem intensely real to whomever has one. But are these experiences reliable guides to the reality of the afterlife?"[16]

To me that's the key question, and it's the one I want to focus on in the following chapters. Let's get started.

CHAPTER 3

"I THOUGHT I'D DIED AND GONE TO HEAVEN"

We should never ask of anything "Is it real?" . . . The proper question is
"A real what?"

C. S. LEWIS

TALES OF TRIPS to heaven and back are intriguing, and millions today find them inspiring. People are drawn to them like bugs to a light. Readers can't seem to get enough of them. Millions desperately want to believe what these books vividly describe about life beyond this life. But should we? Are these books reliable guides? Should we take what they say about heaven at face value?

The only way to know for sure whether these books are credible is to examine their claims in light of God's Word. In chapter 7, we'll consider these books' main assertions and some of the foundational concerns they raise. But before we get to that point, we have to make sure we understand what they're saying. So, in the next four chapters, I want to briefly survey some of the bestselling, landmark books in this burgeoning genre.

The heaven-and-back phenomenon burst on the scene in the early 1990s. In the years that followed, three groundbreaking books brought heaven down to earth. They opened the door to heaven that many after them have claimed to pass through. In this chapter I want to examine what these first three books purport to tell us about heaven and life after death, followed by a brief assessment of their claims. I think you'll be surprised.

Embraced by the Light

By all accounts the beginning of the modern era of near-death experiences (NDEs) occurred in 1975 with the publication of Raymond Moody's bestseller *Life After Life*, but the first heaven-and-back account to capture the public's attention was *Embraced by the Light* by Betty J. Eadie. *Embraced by the Light* is the seminal book about a visit to heaven and back. Released in 1992, the book catapulted to the top of the *New York Times* Best Sellers List. It remained on the list for over two years, sold millions of copies, and was translated into over thirty-five languages. When I checked recently, the book was still selling very well on Amazon.com, more than twenty years after its initial publication.

Eadie, a mother of seven at age thirty-one, claims she died after hemorrhaging while recovering from a hysterectomy in 1973 in a Seattle hospital. She graphically recounts her experience:

> My spirit was suddenly drawn out through my chest and pulled upward, as if by a giant magnet. My first impression was that I was free. There was nothing unnatural about the experience. I was above the bed, hovering near the ceiling. My sense of freedom was limitless and it seemed as if I had done this forever. I turned and saw a body lying on the bed. I was curious about who it was, and immediately I began descending toward it. Having worked as an LPN, I knew well the appearance of a dead body, and as I got closer to the face I knew at once that it was lifeless. And then I recognized that it was my own. That was *my* body on the bed. I wasn't taken aback, and I wasn't frightened; I simply felt a kind of sympathy for it. It appeared younger and prettier than I remembered, and now it was dead.[1]

Betty Eadie identifies herself as a Christian and frequently mentions Jesus. Her book is dedicated "To The Light, my Lord and Savior Jesus Christ." She says, "Of all knowledge, however, there is none more essential than knowing Jesus Christ. I was told that he is the door through which we will *all* return. He is the only door through which we can return. Whether we learn of Jesus Christ here or while in the spirit, we must eventually accept him and surrender to his love."[2]

Statements like this make the book more palatable for an undiscerning Christian audience, but in my opinion they make the book much more dangerous. Her Christian profession is undermined by the many contradictions between her book and *the* book—the Bible.

Embraced by the Light has been thoroughly critiqued over the years, with commenters noting Eadie's ties to the Church of Jesus Christ of Latter-day Saints and blending of New Age philosophy. William Alnor aptly summarizes these critiques when he characterizes *Embraced by the Light* as "a toxic mix of New Age teachings and mind-science theology, sprinkled with a dose of Mormonism."[3]

For a more thorough exposé of *Embraced by the Light* I recommend *Deceived by the Light* by Doug Groothuis.[4] Groothuis does an excellent job dissecting Eadie's claims in light of Scripture. Here I'll highlight a few of the major problems with Eadie's theology in general and her description of heaven in particular. Eadie's book is horribly flawed and heretical. As such, no Christian should take this book seriously.

Cutting Off the Critics

Eadie makes many claims in her heavenly memoir, but one of her primary propositions is that Jesus taught and instructed her about many things, including the mysteries of the universe. While in heaven, she immediately understood things that had always puzzled her. In one sobering statement, she extols the knowledge she received, a claim that borders on attaining omniscience (knowing all things) for herself. She writes, "The word 'omniscient' had never been more meaningful to me. Knowledge permeated me. In a sense it *became* me, and I was amazed at my ability to comprehend the mysteries of the universe simply by reflecting on them."[5] Her claim to omniscience seems to be an attempt to short-circuit any criticism of her aberrant views.

At another point, she asks Jesus why there are so many churches and religions:

> I wanted to know why there were so many churches in the world. Why didn't God give us only one church, one pure religion? The answer came to me with the purest of understanding. Each of us, I was told, is at a different level of spiritual development and understanding. Each person is therefore prepared for a different level of spiritual knowledge. All religions upon the earth are necessary because there are people who need what they teach. People in one religion may not have a complete understanding of the Lord's gospel and never will have while in that religion. But that religion is used as a stepping stone to further knowledge. Each church fulfills spiritual needs that perhaps others cannot fill. No one church can fulfill everybody's needs at every level. As an individual raises his level of understanding about God and his own eternal progress, he might feel discontented with the teachings of his present church

and seek a different philosophy or religion to fill that void. When this occurs he has reached another level of understanding and will long for further truth and knowledge, and for another opportunity to grow. And at every step of the way, these new opportunities to learn will be given. Having received this knowledge, I knew that we have no right to criticize any church or religion in any way. They are all precious and important in his sight.[6]

This undercuts Jesus' uniqueness and the enormity of his sacrifice. Jesus claimed that "no one can come to the Father except through me" (John 14:6). Why would Jesus, who died for his church and left us with his inspired, inerrant Word, tell someone that differing views of truth are equally acceptable? In his last words to the church in Revelation 2–3, Jesus left no doubt that he is dead serious about the creed and conduct of his churches. Any purported revelation to the contrary is false.

Pre-mortal Existence

Embraced by the Light takes several strange twists, but one of the most shocking is when Eadie talks about the pre-mortal or preexistence of souls. She believes humans didn't originate on earth. "The fact of a pre-earth life crystallized in my mind, and I saw that death was actually a 'rebirth' into a greater life of understanding and knowledge that stretched forward and backward through time."[7] She amplifies this thought several times in the book:

> All people as spirits in the pre-mortal world took part in the creation of the earth. We were thrilled to be part of it. We were with God, and we knew that he created us, that we were his very own children. . . . Each spirit who was to come to earth assisted in planning the conditions on earth, including the laws of mortality which would govern us. . . . We assisted God in the development of plants and animal life that would be here. . . . I saw that in the pre-mortal world we knew about and even chose our missions in life. I understood that our stations in life are based upon the objectives of those missions. Through divine knowledge we knew what many of our tests and experiences would be, and we prepared accordingly. We bonded with others—family members and friends—to help us complete our missions. . . . Then we watched as the earth was created. We watched as our spirit brothers and sisters entered physical bodies for their turns upon the earth.[8]

There is nothing in the Bible that even remotely corroborates Eadie's notion of the pre-mortal existence of souls. When God breathed into Adam's nostrils, he "became a living soul" (Genesis 2:7, KJV). His soul came into existence at that point, not in some prior existence. The same is true of every human. God creates the soul. The Bible teaches that a human comes into existence at the moment of physical conception (see Psalm 139:13-16; Zechariah 12:1). When the Bible speaks of God "knowing" a person before they are born (see Isaiah 49:1; Jeremiah 1:5), this does not refer to spiritual existence before birth but rather means that God knows his plans for a person before he or she exists. As an architect knows a building and its purpose before the foundation is laid, God knows us before we're born. The only human being who existed spiritually before conception is Jesus Christ (see John 1:1, 14). In claiming every human being existed spiritually before conception, Eadie diminishes the uniqueness of Jesus.[9]

Appearing on the program *20/20* in 1994, Eadie said, "I learned that we are all divine by nature. Each and every one of us is divine. Perfect. When we come down to earth we become mutated."[10] By touting humanity's divinity and downplaying Christ's, Eadie is peddling egregious error.

Second-Chance Salvation

Eadie's stark divergence from biblical truth doesn't end with pre-mortal existence. She also believes in postmortem salvation—that is, an opportunity for all people to accept Christ after death. She says,

> Because of lack of knowledge or belief, some spirits are virtual prisoners of this earth. Some who die as atheists, or those who have bonded to the world through greed,

bodily appetites, or other earthly commitments find it
difficult to move on, and they become earth-bound.
They often lack the faith and power to reach for, or in
some cases even to recognize, the energy and light that
pulls us toward God. These spirits stay on the earth
until they learn to accept the greater power around
them and to let go of the world. . . . They reside
there as long as they want to in its love and warmth,
accepting its healing influence, but eventually they
learn to move on to accept the greater warmth and
security of God. . . . Whether we learn of Jesus Christ
here or while in the spirit, we must eventually accept
him and surrender to his love.[11]

Jesus says the opposite. "Work hard to enter the narrow
door to God's Kingdom, for many will try to enter but will
fail. When the master of the house has locked the door, it will
be too late. You will stand outside knocking and pleading,
'Lord, open the door for us!' But he will reply, 'I don't know
you or where you come from'" (Luke 13:24-25). These words
of Jesus tell us that some who want to get into God's heavenly
Kingdom will be denied access. Why? Because they're too
late. The Bible says, "It is appointed for man to die once, and
after that comes judgment" (Hebrews 9:27, ESV). The Bible
knows nothing of a second-chance, postmortem opportunity
for eternal life. After death we face judgment, not another
chance to get it right.

As Phil Ryken states, "People do not come back from

death and then choose a different destiny. The life we have for making our kingdom choice is this life, and not the life to come. Our eternal state, said the Scottish theologian Thomas Boston, is determined by our relationship to Christ at the moment when death 'will open the doors of heaven or hell' to us."[12] Ryken continues:

> Jesus tells us to strive to enter by the narrow door. Salvation is a limited-time offer. No gospel will be preached in hell. By then it will be too late to repent, too late to believe, and too late to enter the kingdom of God. So the question is not how many doors there are. God knows there is only one. The question is whether we will enter the one and only door while we still have the time. Don't miss the kingdom of God![13]

The Sovereignty of Man

Another of Eadie's many mistakes is her repeated lowering of God's power and raising of man's profile. Eliminating the sovereignty of God and elevating the will of man, she says, "Our own actions determine the course of our lives, and we can alter or redirect our lives at any time. I understood that this was crucial; God made the promise that he wouldn't intervene in our lives *unless we asked him*."[14] This flies in the face of the entirety of Scripture. God intervenes as he chooses. He doesn't wait for human invitation to act. He intervened in Job's life dramatically without Job's asking by allowing Satan to afflict Job. The global flood was a major unrequested intervention. The Babylonian exile of Judah and all God's discipline of Israel in the Old Testament was strong intervention by a sovereign, covenant-keeping God.

Another illustration of Eadie's belief in pre-mortal existence combines with her lofty view of human choice and free will. She writes that "spirits can choose to enter their mother's body at any stage of her pregnancy. Once there, they immediately begin experiencing mortality."[15] According to Eadie, we exist before we're conceived, and the choice is ours of when we enter the womb. In essence we become the sovereigns in place of God. We are cocreators with him.

She further believes that "at the time of death, we are given the choice to remain on this earth until our bodies are buried or to move on, as I did, to the level to which our spirit had grown."[16] The apostle Paul, by contrast, writes that the souls of believers go immediately to be with the Lord (see 2 Corinthians 5:8). In the story of the Rich Man and Lazarus in Luke 16, Jesus gives no indication of a human choice about when our soul moves on.

Much more could be said about the heretical errors in *Embraced by the Light*, but as with almost all the heaven-and-back books, Eadie mixes biblical references and popular Christian terminology with her alleged new revelation from heaven. John MacArthur aptly describes Eadie's worldview as "universalist reincarnationist self-deificationist ideas."[17] Eadie's book is filled with errant, bizarre teachings and is dangerous to the undiscerning, who could easily be swept away by its compelling story. Believers should soundly reject Eadie's book and warn others to steer clear of it as well.

A Divine Revelation of Heaven

After Betty Eadie's book, the next bestselling account of a heavenly sojourn was Mary K. Baxter's *A Divine Revelation of Heaven*. Mrs. Baxter, an ordained minister, says she had visions of both heaven and hell. In *A Divine Revelation of Hell* she claims that Jesus took her on numerous trips to hell over a thirty-day period in 1976 (we will discuss *A Divine Revelation of Hell* in chapter 8). The odysseys to hell began during the Easter season and occurred from two o'clock to five o'clock in the morning. Her terrible tour of hell was followed by a series of ten trips to heaven, recorded in *A Divine Revelation of Heaven*.

What distinguishes Baxter's books from most of the others in this genre is that her alleged journeys to heaven and hell did not occur in conjunction with an NDE. She was not near death when the trips to heaven and hell occurred. She was asleep in bed when most of the encounters occurred but also received some visions while she was in "deep prayer, meditation and worship."[18] What allegedly happened to her could be described as visions or personal visits to heaven and the underworld.

A Divine Revelation of Heaven is repetitive and at times a bit disjointed. As I read Baxter's book, I got the feeling she was rehearsing the same information over and over. The book is filled with hokey, "canned" descriptions of heaven such as the "room of tears," where all human tears are stored, and the "room of records," where meticulous records are kept in books by busy angels. Larry Dixon describes her visions of heaven as "more like a sad grade-B movie, missing the essence and subtlety of the original script."[19]

On a more positive note, Baxter appears to have a sincere interest in the salvation of the lost. Her book is filled with earnest appeals for the reader to repent of sin and turn to the Lord for salvation. While this is commendable, her view of salvation seems confused in places and at times comes close to teaching salvation by good works.

Inspired or Inaccurate?

One of the brashest claims in Baxter's book is in the foreword by Dr. T. L. Lowery. He writes in glowing terms, "The inspired writings of Mary Kathryn Baxter are divinely anointed by God."[20] That's quite a claim for him to make. Yet Baxter seems also to put her writing on equal footing with the Bible when she says, "Read chapters 3 and 14 of the Gospel of John. And please read this book [referring to her own] from cover to cover so you can understand more about hell and the hereafter."[21] She boldly proclaims, "The Spirit of the living God revealed to me everything I am telling you."[22] These claims are no doubt made to bolster the credibility of the book, but they also invite additional scrutiny. As Christians, we believe the Bible is the uniquely inspired Word of God.

Name It and Claim It

Baxter also uses her visit to heaven to reinforce and promote her views of various theological issues, especially her view of divine healing. At one point, she claims to see a wall with the word *Storehouse* etched on top of it. An angel tells her that the rooms in the storehouse "contained blessings that are stored up for God's people. . . . Healings are waiting for people on earth. The day will come when there will be an avalanche of miracles and healings on the earth. . . . The blessings contained here await the belief of those on earth. All they have to do is believe and receive."[23] She says, "Children of God, don't you know that God wants to do miracles today just as He did yesterday?"[24] The "believe and receive" or "name it and claim it" viewpoint pervades Baxter's book on heaven as well as the book about her alleged visit to hell.

Baxter later asserts, "[God] also wants us to be healed now. . . . God doesn't desire that we spend our later years bedridden and ineffective. . . . There are storehouses of unclaimed blessings in heaven. They are ready to be claimed by God's people who ask in faith—and in the name of Jesus."[25] Baxter's agenda to advocate divine healing for all who believe doesn't square with Scripture. The apostle Paul was given a "thorn in [the] flesh" and prayed three times for the Lord to remove it, yet the Lord did not (see 2 Corinthians 12:7). Are we willing to say that Paul didn't have enough faith to be healed? Ironically, Paul was given the thorn in the flesh to keep him from becoming proud because he was given a revelation of heaven. On one occasion, Paul left his friend

Trophimus sick in the city of Miletus and went on ahead without him (see 2 Timothy 4:20), and Paul told Timothy to drink some wine for his stomach problems and frequent ailments (see 1 Timothy 5:23). Did Timothy and Trophimus also lack the faith to be healed?

Of course, God can and does heal his people at times according to his sovereign will and from his heart of grace and compassion. But the teaching that God wills for every believer to be healed at all times by simply asking in faith is not taught in the New Testament, so Baxter's vision seems to have a shaky foundation.

Going beyond What Is Written

Baxter quotes Scripture liberally and relates it to what she claims to have seen in heaven, yet she goes far beyond God's Word in many places and reflects no apparent fear or hesitancy whatsoever adding to the scriptural information about heaven. The information flows with impunity. She includes all kinds of details. Despite the biblical authors' choice to not describe Jesus' appearance, she says he "seemed to me to be about six feet tall. His beard appeared as if it had been neatly trimmed. His thick hair rested lightly on His shoulders. His beautiful eyes were piercing."[26] Larry Dixon writes, "The reserve and reticence of the Bible to describe heaven and hell is replaced by Baxter's detailed description of both realms."[27]

At the end of her book about her visit to hell, Baxter recounts a vision of heaven God gave her near the end of her journey through hell:

I received this heavenly vision while in deep prayer, meditation and worship. The glory of the Lord descended upon the place where I was praying. Great billows of fire, bright lights and majestic power came before my eyes. In the center of the fire and the lights was the throne of God. On the throne was a similarity of God. Joy, peace and love flowed from God Almighty. The air around the throne was filled with baby cherubim, singing and kissing the Lord upon His face, His hands and His feet. The song they sang was "Holy, holy, holy is the Lord God Almighty." The cherubim had tongues of fire sitting on their heads and on the tips of each tiny wing. The motion of their wings seemed synchronized with the movement of the power and glory of the Lord.[28]

Clearly this is taken from the Great Throne description in Revelation 4, yet Baxter freely adds to the inspired account of John that there were "baby cherubim" around the throne who are "kissing the Lord upon His face." Their kissing the Lord on the face contradicts their repeated adoration—"Holy, holy, holy"—which means "separate, separate, separate" or "other, other, other." God is separate or other from all creation. Beings in the presence of the thrice-holy God wouldn't kiss him on the face. Baxter shows little restraint, consistently adding to God's Word about heaven and violating the biblical injunction in 1 Corinthians 4:6 to "not go beyond what is written" (NIV).

Much more could and has been said about Baxter's book on heaven, but I will leave you with this thought from Larry Dixon: "Paul says the glories of heaven are indescribable. Mrs. Baxter takes 205 pages to describe those glories. Paul got a 'thorn in the flesh' for his revelations; all Mrs. Baxter appears to get are speaking engagements and book tours."[29]

90 Minutes in Heaven

The next bestselling book about a trip to heaven and back was *90 Minutes in Heaven* by Don Piper in 2004. What sets this book apart is that the author is an ordained Baptist pastor. The book sold millions of copies, hitting the *New York Times* Best Sellers List.

Piper's alleged trip to heaven and back occurred after a devastating car accident on January 18, 1989, as he was returning from a conference. His car was crushed under the wheels of a truck, and medical attendants pronounced him dead at the scene. Ninety minutes after he was pronounced dead, a Baptist preacher prayed over Piper's lifeless body, and he came back to life. During the ninety-minute period he was pronounced dead, Piper believes he went to heaven:

> When I died, I didn't flow through a long, dark tunnel. I had no sense of fading away or of coming back. I never felt my body being transported into the light. I heard no voices calling to me or anything else. Simultaneous with my last recollection of

seeing the bridge and the rain, a light enveloped me, with a brilliance beyond earthly comprehension or description. Only that.

In my next moment of awareness, I was standing in heaven.[30]

He claims that upon arrival, he was immediately met by a reception committee in heaven and that he met his grandfather, childhood friend, great-grandfather, and great-grandmother. In his memories of paradise Piper says he saw the gates of heaven and made it up to them but never went in. (So perhaps his book is misnamed.) He was swept back to earth before he had time to go through the gates into heaven itself. Piper's description of heaven is much more brief and less detailed than other more recent books. Only about fifteen of the book's two hundred pages describe his time in the suburbs of glory. In this section Piper recounts what he saw and felt:

Everything I saw glowed with intense brightness. The best I can describe it is that we began to move toward that light. No one said it was time to do so, and yet we all started forward at the same time. . . . I wasn't blinded, but I was amazed that the luster and intensity continually increased. Strange as it seems, as brilliant as everything was, each time I stepped forward, the splendor increased. The farther I walked, the brighter the light. The light engulfed me, and I had the sense that I was being ushered into the presence of God. Although our earthly eyes must gradually adjust to light or darkness, my heavenly eyes saw with absolute ease.[31]

Piper claims that his most vivid memory of heaven is what he heard. He describes it as "a holy swoosh of wings" that would have to be magnified "thousands of times to explain the effect of the sound in heaven."[32] His most troubling statement comes in his description of music in the corridors of heaven:

Many of the old hymns and choruses I had sung at various times in my life were part of the music— along with hundreds of songs I had never heard before. . . . As I stood before the gate, I didn't think of it, but later I realized that I didn't hear such songs as "The Old Rugged Cross" or "The Nail-Scarred Hand." None of the hymns that filled the air were about Jesus' sacrifice or death. I heard no sad songs and instinctively knew that there are no sad songs in heaven. Why would there be? All were praises about Christ's reign as King of Kings and our joyful worship for all he has done for us and how wonderful he is.[33]

Piper's depiction of heavenly music is strangely at odds with the biblical description of singing in heaven. Revelation

5:8-12 gives us a glimpse of glory and the praise of the Lamb around the throne:

> When he took the scroll, the four living beings and
> the twenty-four elders fell down before the Lamb.
> Each one had a harp, and they held gold bowls filled
> with incense, which are the prayers of God's people.
> And they *sang a new song* with these words:
>
> "You are worthy to take the scroll
> and break its seals and open it.
> *For you were slaughtered, and your blood has ransomed
>   people for God*
> from every tribe and language and people and nation.
> And you have caused them to become
> a Kingdom of priests for our God.
> And they will reign on the earth."
>
> Then I looked again, and I heard the voices of
> thousands and millions of angels around the throne
> and of the living beings and the elders. And they
> sang in a mighty chorus:
>
> "Worthy is the Lamb *who was slaughtered*—
> to receive power and riches
> and wisdom and strength
> and honor and glory and blessing." (emphasis mine)

MARK HITCHCOCK || 49

Like the other books in this genre, I believe Piper's portrayal of heaven fails the biblical measure of accuracy. His description about music in heaven doesn't square with Scripture. Revelation tells us heaven is filled with songs of praise for the sacrificial death of the Lord Jesus. If Piper failed in something as simple as accurately relating details about music in heaven, how can we trust the rest of his account? Added to this is the same problem that plagues all of these books—going beyond what the Bible tells us about heaven. Piper, like all the others, believes that his memoir can tell us more about heaven and fill in some of the missing details from the Bible. For me this is the overarching problem with his book and all the others in this genre.

Piper's story of his recovery on earth after the accident is compelling. He spent 105 days in the hospital and endured an agonizing rehabilitation. His patient endurance in suffering is admirable. Also, to his credit, Piper, unlike most of the "trip to heaven books," does clearly state the gospel of Jesus Christ. He believes that the only way to heaven is through personal faith in the death, burial, and resurrection of Jesus Christ (see 1 Corinthians 15:1-3). I'm thankful for his faithfulness to the good news of God's grace through Jesus Christ, but that faithfulness does not lessen my concerns about his misstatement concerning the music that's heard in heaven and his lack of awareness that adding to the Bible's information about heaven is contrary to Scripture. As significant as these three groundbreaking books were for the new genre of heaven-and-back books, we soon discovered they were a pregame warm-up for what began in the late 2000s.

CHAPTER 4

YOUR BEST AFTERLIFE NOW

I've never been to heaven, but I've been to Oklahoma.

THREE DOG NIGHT

THE GROUNDBREAKING BOOKS in the visits-to-heaven genre spanned a twelve-year period from 1992 to 2004. While this wave of heaven-and-back books enjoyed brisk sales, it's almost insignificant compared to the tsunami that hit a few years later. Beginning in the early 2000s, the heavenly flood-gates were opened. As we saw in chapter 1, dozens and dozens of "I've been to heaven and back" stories have rolled off the press—and probably scores more that I haven't seen. While many of these books could be considered and critiqued, and some are much more dangerous than others, in this chap-ter I want to focus on two of the bestselling heaven-and-back books—books millions of people have read—Crystal

McVea's *Waking Up in Heaven* and Kevin Malarkey's *The Boy Who Came Back from Heaven.*

Waking Up in Heaven

Of all the books about trips to heaven and back, *Waking Up in Heaven* is the most interesting to me. Crystal McVea, who is from my home state of Oklahoma, grew up in a chaotic, dysfunctional family. *Waking Up in Heaven: A True Story of Brokenness, Heaven, and Life Again* tells the wrenching saga of sexual abuse (beginning at age three), family chaos, and her own divorce and abortion of a child. Her story includes her marriage to her husband, Virgil. The love and appreciation she has for her husband and children is encouraging. *That* story is worth telling. Her description of her alleged trip to heaven is not. There is a great deal of helpful narrative in *Waking Up in Heaven* of our need for salvation and forgiveness of sins, but the presentation of the gospel in the book is contradictory and confusing at best.

The account of Crystal McVea's alleged trip to heaven begins in 2009, when she was being treated for pancreatitis and suffered an unexpected reaction to pain medication that caused her to stop breathing. She says her heart quit beating, and she stopped breathing for nine minutes. When her eyes shut on earth, she claims she opened her eyes in heaven. However, she's not certain if she died or not. McVea says, "Did I actually die? That's also hard to say. I couldn't breathe, and I had no pulse. . . . Still, I always tell people that I died and came back. I'm not a doctor and I don't know if technically that is 100 percent right, but I do know I was no longer in my human body. I know without any doubt that I passed on to another world."[1] Like all the other heaven-and-back books, McVea says that human words cannot describe what she saw, yet she does her best to do so in vivid detail. Let's consider her claims.

Self-Discovery

First, her purported odyssey to heaven begins with a rather shocking statement in light of Scripture. She claims she left her body behind and was in spirit form. Then she says, "I was flooded with self-knowledge, and all the junk that cluttered my identity on Earth instantly fell away, revealing, for the first time ever, the real me. . . . Imagine that—the first person we meet in heaven is ourselves."[2] Later, she says, "And so, for the first time ever, I was filled with love for myself. How could I not love myself? I was God's perfect creation!"[3]

There's a great deal in the book about McVea's feelings and how she felt in heaven. She describes not only seeing God but how she was feeling him. Overall her descriptions are supremely self-centered, not God-centered, which is in stark contrast to the biblical descriptions of heaven. When Ezekiel, Isaiah, and John describe their visions of heaven, there is nothing about their love for themselves or their own worthiness before God. To the contrary, they are shaken to the core, undone, and left stunned by God's majesty and glory.

Commenting on books about trips to heaven, John MacArthur says,

> The current best-selling heavenly travelogues all have one disturbing tendency in common: they manage to make the heavenly tourist seem heroic while making heaven itself sound somewhat mundane. . . . They say comparatively little about the glory of God, the very centerpiece of heaven. But all of them have a lot to say about how good *they* felt—how peaceful, how happy, how comforted they were; how they received privileges and accolades; how fun and enlightening their experience was; and how many things they think they now understand perfectly that could never be gleaned from Scripture alone. In short, they glorify self while barely noticing God's glory. They highlight everything but what's truly important about heaven."[4]

Sadly, *Waking Up in Heaven* fits this description. There is little to nothing about the glory and greatness of God and a great deal about the author and how she felt. The self-focus is reinforced when McVea gives a detailed account of seeing a little girl about age three or four during her trip to heaven. After a lengthy description of the child, McVea says, "The little girl . . . was me."[5] She refers to this experience several times. One of the most thrilling things about heaven to her is seeing herself as a little girl. This seems to be grossly at odds with what will truly excite us in heaven—seeing and experiencing the glory of God.

Heavenly Hours

Second, McVea states categorically, "In heaven, there are no minutes or hours or days. In heaven, there is no such thing as 'time.'"[6] This statement, which is reiterated in many of the heaven books, is contradicted by two passages about heaven in the book of Revelation. Revelation 6:9-11 says,

> When the Lamb broke the fifth seal, I saw under the altar the souls of all who had been martyred for the word of God and for being faithful in their testimony. They shouted to the Lord and said, "O Sovereign Lord, holy and true, how long before you judge the people who belong to this world and avenge our blood for what they have done to us?" Then a white robe was given to each of them. And they were told to rest a little longer until the full number of their brothers and sisters—their fellow servants of Jesus who were to be martyred—had joined them.

From this passage we can see that these martyrs in heaven clearly have some concept of the passage of time. The Lord even tells them to rest for "a little longer," which indicates that there is time. And again, in Revelation 8:1, the apostle John, who is transported to the future in a spiritual state, says, "When the Lamb broke the seventh seal on the scroll, there was silence throughout heaven for about half an hour." Of course, this could be speaking of the passage of time from John's frame of reference on earth as he saw the glorious vision of the blowing of the heavenly trumpets. But it seems to me that it refers to the passage of time in heaven. McVea's statement that there's no time in heaven seems to fly in the face of how heaven is described in the book of Revelation.

Should I Stay or Should I Go?

A third concern with McVea's story is that the choice was completely up to her whether to stay in heaven or return to earth.[7] If that's true, why doesn't everyone make the choice to come back? One would think people would be coming back from heaven all the time if that were true. Wouldn't many mothers and fathers want to come back to finish raising their children if they were given the choice? Does the sovereign God really place the choice of whether people stay in heaven or go back to earth in their hands? Again, this is a very human-centered view of heaven and eternity.

There's no evidence in the Bible that God ever gives someone a choice about whether to stay in heaven or come back to earth. God claims that he is completely sovereign over life and death. "Look now; I myself am he! There is no other god but me! I am the one who kills and gives life; I am the one who wounds and heals; no one can be rescued from my powerful hand" (Deuteronomy 32:39). Jesus says, "I am the living one. I died, but look—I am alive forever and ever! And

I hold the keys of death and the grave" (Revelation 1:18). Jesus claims the prerogative of life and death for himself. McVea's view attempts to bypass the sovereign choice of God.

Feelings and Faith

Fourth, in the later part of the book, McVea recounts numerous times she was able to tell others her story about going to heaven and back. People she meets are enamored of her story of heaven and eager to hear about it. She speaks mostly about God's love and what it "felt like to be with God." Others are instantly drawn to her message. In a few of her examples she does go a bit deeper. She quotes Ephesians 2:8-9, which is a great statement of God's grace in saving sinners: "God saved you by his grace when you believed. And you can't take credit for this; it is a gift from God. Salvation is not a reward for the good things we have done, so none of us can boast about it." Near the end of the book she quotes Colossians 2:13-14, another beautiful gospel passage: "You were dead because of your sins and because your sinful nature was not yet cut away. Then God made you alive with Christ, for he forgave all our sins. He canceled the record of the charges against us and took it away by nailing it to the cross."

At one point she says, "*This* was why He sent me back. *This* was why He had me tell my whole story. If a sinner like me could be forgiven, then *anyone* could be forgiven. God loves all His children, each and every one. This was the message my story was meant to convey."[8]

But McVea never really gets specific about how we're

forgiven. The message of the cross of Jesus Christ and the empty tomb is never given its preeminent place.

The book closes with these words: "You don't have to die and go to heaven. All you have to do to be in God's presence is choose Him. All you have to do is believe."[9] This sounds good, but it leaves the reader with one question: believe in what, or believe in whom? The reader is left with a nebulous statement about believing, but faith is only as good as its object. A person can believe wholeheartedly that a chair will hold him or her up, but if the chair is weak, it will give way under the weight. On the other hand, a person may have slender faith in the chair, but if it is strong enough to hold the weight, then that person is secure. The object of faith is the key. All the faith in the world in the wrong object is worthless. Faith in Jesus Christ is the only faith that will save.

During one of her presentations, McVea related how a seventy-five-year-old woman who had been molested as a child was convinced that God loved her and said, "'Now I know God *does* love me! God has loved me all along.' The woman gave her life to Jesus Christ that day, and she was changed."[10]

I appreciate these stories and realize that God can use imperfect means to save people. I pray that people really have come to know Christ as Savior and Lord through Crystal McVea's ministry. However, in many of the conversations she includes in the book, she never communicates the one requirement for entrance into heaven—namely, faith and trust in Jesus Christ as Savior from sin. This is an astounding omission for someone who claims to have gone to heaven.

Like most of the alleged heavenly visitors, she reports that as a result of her visit, she was liberated from all the baggage she carried throughout her life, that she got rid of her grudges and grievances against others, that she became much less attached to material things, and that a lifetime of doubt was replaced by the assurance that she was "a loving child of God." She states, "Yes, God gave me the miraculous gift of His presence and His wisdom, and because of my time in heaven I now overflow with excitement and passion for Him. The love I felt pass between us changed me forever. I am beyond lucky to have had this experience, and I can't even imagine what my life would be like if I hadn't."[11] While changes like these are certainly positive, they don't prove the reliability of her report, especially in light of the superficial, human-centered nature of her account of the glories of heaven.

The Message

The most troubling message from *Waking Up in Heaven* is its summary statement. Near the end of the book, McVea says,

> I share the message God sent me back to share. And what is that message? It is many things, but here is one way I would put it: *God is real, and we are all worthy of His love and salvation because He finds us worthy.* That may sound simple, but for me it

changed everything. It was the answer I had spent
so much time trying to find. And now that I have it,
the fondest wish I have in my heart is for everyone—
everyone—to have it, too. I want everyone to be
there with me. . . . We are, all of us, God's perfect
creations, and we are so worthy of His love.[12]

Reading this statement shocks me, and I hope it shocks
you. It sounds more like a popular self-help slogan than the
gospel of God's grace to undeserving sinners. Moreover, it
contradicts or at least confuses what McVea says elsewhere
in the book about her being a sinner in need of forgiveness.
The message of the true gospel is not "I am worthy" but "*He*
is worthy—I am unworthy, and Christ alone is worthy." I
understand that McVea is not a theologian and doesn't claim
to be, but she says this is the message God sent her back to
share. I have to wonder why God would send someone back
from heaven to share a message on earth that contradicts or
at best confuses what he says throughout the New Testament.

Any person who has read Scripture and trusted in Jesus
Christ for forgiveness and eternal life should know that we are
not worthy of his love and salvation. Our unworthiness is what
makes salvation and forgiveness necessary. Jesus said that those
who admit their unworthiness and desperate need for forgiveness are those who are justified before God (see Luke 18:9-14).
McVea's summary statement turns the gospel on its head.

God's Word portrays the plight of people without Christ
in the strongest terms. Ephesians 2:1-3 says, "Once you were

dead because of your disobedience and your many sins. You used to live in sin, just like the rest of the world, obeying the devil—the commander of the powers in the unseen world. . . . All of us used to live that way, following the passionate desires and inclinations of our sinful nature. By our very nature we were subject to God's anger, just like everyone else." Romans 3:10-12 is no more flattering about the human condition apart from Christ: "No one is righteous—not even one. No one is truly wise; no one is seeking God. All have turned away; all have become useless. No one does good, not a single one."

The emphasis in Scripture is not on our worthiness but on God's action on our behalf to save us. Romans 5:8-10 says, "God showed his great love for us by sending Christ to die for us while we were still sinners. And since we have been made right in God's sight by the blood of Christ, he will certainly save us from God's condemnation. For since our friendship with God was restored by the death of his Son while we were still his enemies, we will certainly be saved through the life of his Son." Second Corinthians 5:21 says, "God made Christ, who never sinned, to be the offering for our sin, so that we could be made right with God through Christ."

The whole point of the gospel message is that we aren't worthy. If I am worthy and God finds me worthy of his love, then why did the Son of God have to die in my place on the cross as my substitute? If someone has really been to heaven, the main thing she should want people to know is how to get there, and she should be able to correctly point the way. Unfortunately, *Waking Up in Heaven*, while better than most of the other heaven books, is mired in human-centeredness and confuses and clouds the precious gospel message. For these reasons, *Waking Up in Heaven* fails to measure up against the plumb line of biblical scrutiny.

The Boy Who Came Back from Heaven

Kevin Malarkey wrote *The Boy Who Came Back from Heaven* about his son Alex's NDE. It bears a great deal of similarity to Todd Burpo's story about his son in *Heaven Is for Real* (which I will discuss in chapter 6), except Alex Malarkey's injuries are much more serious and debilitating. The story begins with a tragic car accident in November 2004 as Kevin and his oldest child, Alex (age six), were returning from church. Kevin's wife, Beth, had just given birth to their fourth child and was at home with the other three children.

At a dangerous, unfamiliar intersection, Kevin's car was slammed broadside. Alex suffered severe neck trauma. Kevin describes the gruesome injury: "The first vertebra below his skull had been pulled apart from the second and stood at a forty-five-degree angle. . . . He had suffered an internal decapitation—his skull was detached from his spinal column. Skin, muscle, and ligaments were holding his head on his body. . . . The X-ray clearly reveals Alex's vertebrae detached from his head."[13] The gripping story of Alex's paralysis, survival, and long road to recovery is moving. Thankfully, Alex is now free of a ventilator, although he is still confined to a wheelchair.

Malarkey includes a moving scene of Alex's salvation experience as a very young child through faith in Jesus Christ. He also mentions Alex's love for church. Malarkey records these words from Alex: "I want people to understand that Heaven isn't a place where you go just because you do good things. You have to ask Jesus into your heart and ask for forgiveness."[14] For me, these points were highlights in the book. However, as good and true as they are, they don't absolve Malarkey of responsibility for the misleading claims he makes throughout the rest of the book.

Berean Call

Near the conclusion of the book, Malarkey offers several wise principles: "If I may offer a humble word of exhortation, the enemy is a deceiver who masquerades as an angel of light. We all need to be on guard against counterfeit truth. Anything that doesn't square with Scripture is counterfeit. . . . Don't be derailed in your quest for meaning by seeking a supernatural experience. Seek God through His Son, Jesus Christ."[15] He also says, "Fortunately we have the Scriptures as an infallible guide to evaluate everything we experience."[16]

These statements are very good, and I agree with them. They're consistent with Luke's commendation of the Bereans in the book of Acts: "The people of Berea were more open-minded than those in Thessalonica, and they listened eagerly to Paul's message. They searched the Scriptures day after day to see if Paul and Silas were teaching the truth" (17:11).

In spite of these positive statements, at the beginning of

the book, Malarkey implores the reader to defer discernment while reading the book. He says, "I'm not here to beat a drum, convince you of a theological argument, or force you to validate Alex's experiences. But I humbly offer a challenge: suspend your judgment for just a few chapters."[17]

So which is it? Are the Scriptures our infallible guide to "be on guard against counterfeit truth," or do we suspend judgment when we read certain things hoping they're true? Both cannot be done at the same time. Why would someone who believes everything must square with Scripture call on readers to suspend their judgment about what they're reading? One of these principles must ultimately override the other. When Kevin says Alex told him, "There is a hole in outer Heaven. That hole goes to hell," we have to measure this by the Word of God, which never gives even the slightest indication there's a hole in heaven, much less one that goes to hell.[18] When we try to square this—and many other claims in the book—with God's Word, it fails the test.

Father Knows Best?

Beyond questions about the book's conformity to Scripture, serious questions have been raised after its release concerning Alex's support for the book his father has written about his experience. Allegedly Alex posted a negative assessment of his father's story on a webpage publicizing the book, but the comment was quickly removed. Alex's mother, Beth, reposted the comment on her own blog and added, "Buyer beware. There is only one absolutely infallible and 'true' book: God's

Word! It does not need to be fancied up or packaged for sale. It is incredible as it stands."[19] In his book *The Glory of Heaven*, John MacArthur says, "In an email to my editor, Beth Malarkey writes, 'Know that Alex never concluded he was in heaven. He was a small boy who experienced something extraordinary. The adults made it into what would sell to the masses.'"[20]

I have no personal knowledge of the truth of these statements from Alex and Beth, but Beth's adamant non-approval of the book is disturbing, to say the least. One would think that if Alex's experiences are as described in the book, both parents would agree at least on the major details. Beth's statements should give pause to every reader.

The Devil's in the Details

The Boy Who Came Back from Heaven describes the devil and demons at length. Malarkey says Alex told him, "The demons leave when they hear the name of Jesus. Daddy told me about what Jesus taught his followers: 'I have given you authority over all the power of the enemy' (Luke 10:19). So I say, 'Devil—or demons—in Jesus' name, leave my room and leave this house. By the blood of Jesus, I command you to go. Leave me alone.' Once my brother Aaron ended my prayer with, 'Bye-bye, Snake Boy!'"[21]

Malarkey claims that Alex has seen the devil on many occasions. This is difficult for me to believe, since the devil is not omnipresent (everywhere at once). He can only be one place at a time. With all the places on earth where Satan could be at any time working his deception, that he would visit Alex on multiple occasions seems highly unlikely to me. The detailed description of the devil is another unsettling statement:

> The devil is the ugliest thing imaginable. He has three heads. All the heads are the same and have hair on top made of fire. He's got beaming red eyes with flames for pupils, and his nose is nasty and torn up. Each of the heads speaks different lies at the same time. He speaks to me in English, but his voice is screechy like a witch and changes into different sounds.
>
> The devil's mouth is funny looking, with only a few moldy teeth. And I've never noticed any ears.
>
> His body has a human form, with two bony arms and two bony legs. He has no flesh on his body, only some moldy stuff. His robes are torn and dirty.[22]

This portrait of Satan reads like a cartoon caricature. All that's missing are the horns, red suit, and forked tail. The Bible never gives any physical description of Satan. Why is his appearance even relevant? Satan is a spirit being. He can evidently assume some kind of form at times, but the Scripture is devoid of any details about his appearance.

Demons are also described in the book. "Demons are often green. They have hair made of fire, and their skin and robes are just like the devil's, too. The eyes are the same, and demons have long fingernails. Sometimes they're alone, but they're more likely than the devil to attack in groups."[23] These descriptions, likely springing from an overactive imagination, are more like childish caricatures and unworthy of serious consideration.

I Can Only Imagine

In a candid moment, Malarkey expresses his own struggle with doubt about some of Alex's statements. He admits that some of what he has written appears outside the pale and could be attributed to childish imagination:

> From the time of the accident, Alex says, the angels have graced our home. Up to the time he was about eight—the period of Alex's most serious physical struggle—there was a particular group of angels that would surround his bed in our master bedroom.
>
> Alex knew them all by name, and he would carry on conversations with them. John, Vent, and Ryan were names he mentioned. A typical reaction, of course, is to observe that a little boy on a ventilator, who has a baby brother named Ryan, is going to give those names to his imaginary friends. We know that children create imaginary friends to help them cope with new and difficult situations. Passing tedious hours in a wheelchair without the use of anything below his neck would surely inspire a child's imagination as a coping mechanism. Couldn't this

explain these bizarre angel adventures, as well as the suspiciously familiar names? I wrestled with these doubts for a long time.[24]

Malarkey concludes: "In the end, if what we see, hear, or read strains credibility, we must choose whether to believe it. It's not my job to convince you."[25] Malarkey's admission that Alex's situation was fertile soil for an active imagination is telling. If Alex's imagination is the origin of the angelic visits, couldn't it also be the source of the other alleged revelations about heaven as well? I think Malarkey, in this moment of self-revelation, came to the proper conclusion about what was going on. And it's my conclusion as well.

John MacArthur summarizes the matter well: "In short, *The Boy Who Came Back from Heaven* is a study in how human passion unchecked by discernment can give way to blind gullibility. It also illustrates the danger of setting a child's (or anyone's) imagination free in the spiritual realm without proper biblical boundaries. And it shows how subtly and how easily our fallen hearts can breed superstition, pride, and self-deception."[26]

We're all prone to these attitudes, and our only hope is to humbly submit our minds and wills to the Lord and his Word every day.

CHAPTER 5

DEAD WRONG

Everybody wants to go to heaven, but nobody wants to die.

JOE LOUIS

SO FAR WE'VE assessed the heavenly memoirs of three mothers, a Baptist pastor, and a little boy. Their experiences resulted from automobile accidents, serious illnesses, and night visions. No two stories are even close to alike. Adding to this wide diversity, two bestselling heavenly memoirs were written by medical doctors, one male and the other female. Both books were highly acclaimed and created quite a stir when they were released. One of the stories was featured on the cover of *Newsweek*, and the other was the focus of a cover article in *Christianity Today*. No assessment of heaven-and-back books would be complete without considering *To Heaven and Back* and *Proof of Heaven*.

To Heaven and Back

Dr. Mary Neal, an orthopedic doctor from Jackson Hole, Wyoming, authored the number one *New York Times* bestseller *To Heaven and Back: A Doctor's Extraordinary Account of Her Death, Heaven, Angels, and Life Again.* Her story chronicles a near-death experience (NDE) and alleged trip to heaven after she suffered a tragic kayaking accident on the Fuy River in southern Chile in 1999.

It all began when she was pinned in a waterfall, unable to extract herself from the kayak, for almost fifteen minutes. She was finally resuscitated, and the story of her lengthy time of recovery and rehabilitation is moving. The account of her son Willie's death is emotional to read. I can't imagine her heart-wrenching grief. I'm deeply sorry for her loss.

Critiquing a book from someone who has suffered so much is not easy or pleasant. I respect Neal for her endurance in the face of suffering. Her perseverance is admirable. My purpose is not to add to her distress but simply to weigh her account in light of God's unerring Word, which is our only sure guide to the future and life after death. And sadly, her story, like the many others I've already chronicled, falls far short of the mark.

Neal opens by giving an impassioned apologetic for her book. She claims that "it has inspired many people, stimulated discussion, and has often resulted in a rejuvenated relationship with God. It has lessened people's fear of death and increased their passion for living a full and meaningful life. My story has deepened people's faith and given them hope for the future."[1] She claims God sent her back "to tell my story to others and help them find their way back to God."[2] I'm sure Neal is sincere, but the ultimate issue is not whether the book has helped people. Rather, the issue is whether she really went to heaven and came back as she claims. While no one on earth can know for sure if she really went to heaven, we can know that she *didn't* go to heaven if her experience is not in line with God's Word.

Early in the book Neal describes her upbringing and the lack of any clear biblical teaching or exposure in her family. She vaguely relates what she calls her "baptismal spiritual transformation" and is convinced the Holy Spirit descended upon her because when she came out of the water, "I felt light as a feather. I was energized, euphoric, and ecstatic. I felt cleansed and reborn; I became a new person."[3] While this conversion account is long on emotional feelings, there is no mention of her believing in Jesus Christ as her Savior and trusting in him alone for her salvation. While neither I nor anyone else on earth is the final judge concerning the salvation of another person, the Bible is clear that we are born again only by trusting in Jesus alone and believing in him, not by outward ceremonies like baptism (see John 3:36). Anyone's experience must be measured by this standard. Neal does say at one point later in the book, "I renewed my commitment to living a Christ-centered life,"[4] but never really fleshes out what that means.

Dead and Gone

While she was "dead" during her kayaking accident, Neal claims that she went to heaven and was immediately received by a large welcoming committee. Accompanied by these companions, she traveled down a path that led to a "great and brilliant hall" that "represented the last branch point of life, the gate through which each human being must pass."[5] She describes the hall: "It was clear that this hall is the place where each of us is given the opportunity to review our lives and our choices, and where we are each given a final opportunity to choose God or to turn away—for eternity."[6] Neal clearly believes in the possibility of postmortem salvation. Since we addressed this issue earlier (page 36), I won't discuss it again here. But the old maxim is true: "As death finds us, eternity keeps us." Our eternal destiny is settled *before* we die, not after.

The Problem with Preexistence

Like Betty Eadie before her, Neal not only believes that humans have a chance of postmortem salvation, but also maintains that souls exist in a conscious state in heaven prior to conception:

> I need to categorically state, once again, that I
> believe very young children clearly remember where
> they came from and are still quite connected to
> God's world. I believe they easily recall the images,

knowledge, and the love of the world they inhabited before their birth. I believe children may still be able to see angels.[7]

Later, she approvingly quotes one of her friends who said, "Our souls are timeless and come to earth in order to learn something new or otherwise attain spiritual growth."[8] I addressed the notion of preexistence before conception previously (page 34), so I won't repeat the same information here. But John MacArthur says flatly, "The notion that human souls do not originate at conception but exist in a conscious state in heaven prior to being born is not a Christian doctrine."[9]

Neal not only believes that we existed before conception, but she maintains that we had a hand in planning our lives here on earth:

In preparation for our journey to earth, we are able to make a basic outline for our life. This is not to imply that we, the humans, are entirely in charge of our life's design. It is more like God creates it, then we review it and discuss it with our "personal planning" angel. Within the algorithm are written branch points in our lives at which times we may exit, returning to God, or we may be redirected to a different task and goal. We may be directed to these branch points by our own conscious choice and by our circumstances, or we may be pushed along by angelic intervention.[10]

The concept that we review our life plan before our existence with our "personal planning angel" is unbiblical nonsense. There is nothing in the Bible even remotely similar to this. If we had a hand in reviewing our life plan before we were born, most of us would probably wonder sometimes what our prebirth self was thinking in allowing some of life's twists and turns to make it into the final plan. Frankly, if what Neal writes is true, I would like to interview my prebirth self about a couple of points in my algorithm.

"It Is Written"

To Heaven and Back is liberally sprinkled with Scripture to give it a biblical basis and feel of truth, but sometimes the Scriptures are out of context or misinterpreted. For instance, Neal claims when she arrived in heaven she was met by "a group of fifteen to twenty souls (human spirits sent by God)." She says, "This welcoming committee seemed to be wildly cheering for me as I approached the 'finish line.'"[11] She then quotes Hebrews 12:1 as biblical support for this welcoming committee: "Therefore, since we are surrounded by such a huge crowd of witnesses to the life of faith, let us strip off every weight that slows us down, especially the sin that so easily trips us up. And let us run with endurance the race God has set before us." The "huge crowd of witnesses" in Hebrews 12:1 are not people in heaven watching us and welcoming us to heaven. In the context of the passage, the crowd of witnesses are the men and women of faith listed in Hebrews 11 who are witnesses to us as we look back on the power of their lives of faith. We are to look at their lives and emulate their faith in the Lord. They aren't watching *us*; *we* are to be watching *them*.

Ironically, in a book filled with extrabiblical material from trips to heaven and conversations with angels, Neal claims to believe in the Bible and even says that when we're confronted by our own frailty and inability to understand a circumstance or event in life, "our only reasonable option is to rely on the word and promises of God."[12] Yet when it comes to heaven and life after death, she fails to follow her own advice, relying instead upon her own experience that contradicts "the word and promises of God" in several places (like those mentioned above). Why not rely upon the Word and promises of God for everything, including information about the afterlife? Why the need to add to the revelation God has given us about heaven? Isn't God's infallible Word enough? We'll talk more about this in chapter 7.

Faith Is the Victory

As with most of the heaven-and-back books, Neal closes with the main takeaway from her experience. She summarizes, "It is this faith that sets us free. It allows us to fully embrace life, dissolves fear, and replaces worry with hope. Faith allows us to confidently walk with God into a future filled with joy; one that can become an extraordinary and amazing adventure."[13]

But Neal here is wrong. Jesus said, "You will know the truth, and the truth will set you free. . . . If the Son sets you free, you are truly free" (John 8:32, 36). We're set free by the truth concerning the person and work of Jesus Christ. Of course, faith is necessary for us to receive Jesus as our Savior. But faith does not save us. *Jesus* saves us. Faith is the hand that receives him. Faith is the instrumentality or means of salvation but not its basis or cause. Faith is worthless in itself. Again, faith is only as good as its object. All the faith one can muster is worthless if it's in the wrong object.

The nebulous notion of the power of faith leaves the reader with the mistaken idea that as long as you have faith in something, you're in good shape. But even general faith in God is not enough. Even the demons believe in God, yet they have no saving relationship with God through Jesus Christ (see James 2:19). Jesus alone saves (see John 14:6; Acts 4:12). Jesus alone sets us free. The only faith that will bring a soul to heaven is faith in Jesus Christ as Savior and Lord. Someone who claims to have been to heaven and back should know that and clearly tell her readers about it rather than clouding the truth with vague generalizations.

Die Harder, or *Proof of Heaven*

Dr. Eben Alexander is another physician who claims that he visited heaven and has come back to enlighten us about the afterlife. As a highly trained neurosurgeon and self-professed skeptic, Alexander immediately seeks to garner credibility and respect. In 2008, Alexander contracted the E. coli bacteria that invaded his cerebrospinal fluid, producing bacterial meningitis, causing him to slip into a coma. For a period of seven days his entire neocortex (the outer surface of the brain) shut down and was totally inoperative. He maintains that his brain "wasn't working *at all*" and says, "I was allowed to die harder, and travel deeper, than almost all NDE subjects before me."[14] He appeals to his unique condition—an absent neocortex—as definitive proof that he was clinically dead.

The problems with *Proof of Heaven* begin as early as the endorsements. One of the endorsers, Allan J. Hamilton, writes, "*Proof of Heaven* is a compelling story of what may lie ahead for all of us in the life beyond this one. We have nothing to fear."[15] This misleading statement sets the stage for the rest of the book. Categorical statements like this one miss the clear teaching of Scripture that those who fail to trust in Jesus Christ alone for salvation *do* have something to fear when they die. That's one of the grave dangers of books like *Proof of Heaven*: they leave the reader with the clear message that all is well at death for everyone. But Jesus said, "Don't be afraid of those who want to kill your body; they cannot touch your soul. Fear only God, who can destroy both soul and body in hell" (Matthew 10:28). Telling people who do not know Jesus Christ that they have nothing to fear is a lie with eternal consequences. Every person who does not know Christ should fear coming judgment (see Revelation 20:11-15).

Heaven or Hell?

Alexander says his overall experience was "analogous to a dream, in which you remember some things about yourself while forgetting other things completely."[16] Describing the commencement of his alleged saga, he states, "I can't say exactly when it happened, but at a certain point I became aware of some objects around me. . . . I came to call it the Realm of the Earthworm's-Eye View. . . . The longer I stayed in this place, the less comfortable I became."[17] He says, "I wasn't really part of this subterranean world at all, but trapped in it. Grotesque animal faces bubbled out of the muck, groaned or screeched, and then were gone again. I heard an occasional dull roar. . . . Then I became aware of a smell: a little like feces, a little like blood, and a little like vomit. . . . As my awareness sharpened more and more, I edged ever closer to panic. Whoever or whatever I was, I did not belong here. I needed to get out."[18] As I read these words, what struck me is that they sound more like a picture of *hell* than *heaven*.

Alexander finally made it out of wherever he was initially and says he had a companion he refers to as the Orb. He calls God "Om" because that's the sound he remembers hearing associated with God. The place where God dwells Alexander calls "the core," which he describes as a "vast, inky-black core that was the home of the Divine itself . . . black but holy darkness."[19] He repeatedly claims that everything he saw and experienced transcends and bypasses language, yet he continues to try to describe it.

With all due respect, there are so many aberrant views

and unbiblical statements in *Proof of Heaven* that I'm at a loss where to begin. But in order to make it more digestible, I want to focus on four major heresies that Alexander embraces and expounds in this book. Heresies he takes to new heights (pun intended).

Gnosticism

A common thread in the heaven-and-back books is the Gnostic error of claiming that some people can acquire secret knowledge that's inaccessible to the rest of us. This knowledge can come from visions, angelic messengers, dreams, or mystical experiences. Alexander falls into this trap, claiming access to an array of special, hidden information. One example is his secret knowledge of the universe:

> Through the Orb, Om told me that there is not one universe but many—in fact, more than I could conceive—but that love lay at the center of them all. Evil was present in all the other universes as well, but only in the tiniest trace amounts. Evil was necessary because without it free will was impossible, and without free will there could be no growth—no forward movement, no chance for us to become what God longed for us to be. . . . I saw the abundance of life throughout the countless universes, including some whose intelligence was advanced far beyond that of humanity. I saw that there are countless higher dimensions, but that the

only way to know these dimensions is to enter and
experience them directly. They cannot be known,
or understood, from lower dimensional space. . . .
The knowledge given to me was not "taught." . . .
Knowledge was stored without memorization,
instantly and for good. It didn't fade . . . and to this
day I still possess all of it.[20]

This is unadulterated Gnosticism. Alexander claims to
possess deeper knowledge than any of us can fathom. Some
of the things he claims to know are staggering and sensational
but contain various forms of error. He claims to be "in the
know" while the rest of us are left with mere earthly knowledge. Concerning the presence of evil, he states,

Even on earth there is much more good than evil,
but earth is a place where evil is allowed to gain
influence in a way that would be entirely impossible
at higher levels of existence. . . . Small particles of
evil were scattered throughout the universe, but the
sum total of all that evil was as a grain of sand on a
vast beach compared to the goodness, abundance,
hope, and unconditional love in which the universe
was literally awash.[21]

There's a subtle elitism and arrogance that bleeds through
these claims of higher knowledge, not to mention the fact
that this is what people today want to hear. Alexander believes

that others can "glimpse behind the veil" without dying. The only way to gain this glimpse is "we each have to go deep into our own consciousness, through prayer or meditation, to access these truths."[22] Biblical Christianity asserts that the one and only source of transcendent truth is God's Word. It's the only infallible rule for faith and practice (see John 17:17; 2 Timothy 3:15-17; Hebrews 4:12). Scripture is God's written revelation to mankind and is never superseded by man's writings, thoughts, ideas, meditations, or visions no matter how sensational they may appear.

The problem is that Dr. Alexander's avowed secret knowledge contradicts the biblical truth of the very nature of God. Alexander repeatedly references God's love, which is one of the great attributes of God. But he rarely mentions God's holiness and justice. He uses the word *holy* a few times, but never as a prominent feature. Yet the Bible says this is the eternal preoccupation of the beings around God's throne:

> In front of the throne was a shiny sea of glass,
> sparkling like crystal. In the center and around the
> throne were four living beings, each covered with
> eyes, front and back. The first of these living beings
> was like a lion; the second was like an ox; the third
> had a human face; and the fourth was like an eagle
> in flight. Each of these living beings had six wings,
> and their wings were covered all over with eyes,
> inside and out. Day after day and night after night
> they keep on saying, "Holy, holy, holy is the Lord

God, the Almighty—the one who always was, who
is, and who is still to come." (Revelation 4:6-8)

The beings around God's throne don't cry out "love, love,
love," or "grace, grace, grace"; they never stop saying "holy,
holy, holy." The word *holy* means "set apart" or "separate."
What this means is that God is separate from everything
else. God is transcendent in holiness. Throughout the book
Alexander's focus on God's love leads him to make other unbiblical claims such as that "God is present in us at all times.
Omniscient, omnipotent, personal—and loving us without
conditions."[23] This view of God is grossly unbiblical. God
is only present with those who receive his Son. Jesus claims
there is no way to God except through him (see John 14:6).
God does not indwell every person and love them without
conditions. To please God we must have saving faith (see
Hebrews 11:6). Dr. Alexander's "Om" is not the God of the
Bible.

Pantheism

Pantheism is the belief that everything is part of divinity and
the divine is everything. Alexander subscribes to this worldview. He says, "The universe has no beginning or end, and
God is entirely present within every particle of it."[24] This
statement flatly contradicts the Bible, where the universe has
a beginning (see Genesis 1:1) and an ending (see Revelation
21:1). The notion that God is entirely present within every
particle of the universe is blatant pantheism. And Alexander

not only believes *God* is present in everything; he believes *he* is too, at least in his NDE: "The blurring of the boundary between my awareness and the realm around me went so far at times that I became the entire universe."[25]

According to Alexander, "Om is 'human' as well—even *more* human than you and I are."[26] In contrast, the Bible says that "God is Spirit" (John 4:24). Jesus, the second member of the triune Godhead, is uniquely divine and human. He's the God-man. He's man's perfect God and God's perfect man. The sinlessness of Jesus does not mean he is more human than us. Adam and Eve were sinless for a time in the Garden of Eden. Moreover, Alexander never mentions Jesus as being God and man. He says "*Om*" is more human than we are. He never evidences or acknowledges any notion that God is Trinitarian, that is, three persons in one essence or nature. God is not more human than we are. Basic errors about the nature of God and man permeate *Proof of Heaven*.

Mysticism

Proof of Heaven is also mired in mysticism, which is the "belief that union with or absorption into the Deity or the absolute, or the spiritual apprehension of knowledge inaccessible to the intellect, may be attained through contemplation and self-surrender."[27] Simply stated, mysticism is the belief that we have to go beyond our minds to really get in touch with God.

Alexander speaks frequently of existential experiences that supposedly bring one closer to God. "I felt like I was doing what every soul is able to do when they leave their bodies, and what we can all do right now through various methods of prayer or deep meditation."[28]

In another place he says, "Another aspect of the good news is that you don't have to almost die to glimpse behind the veil—but you must do the work. Learning about that realm from books and presentations is a start—but at the end of the day, we each have to go deep into our own consciousness, through prayer or meditation, to access these truths."[29] He goes on to describe a form of "deep conscious exploration" called Hemi-Sync developed by Robert Monroe in the 1950s. In his investigations of this system Monroe claimed to have numerous out-of-body experiences. Alexander touts Hemi-Sync as a system of meditative exercises that allows "access to alternate perceptual modes, including deep meditation and mystical states."[30] Nothing even close to what he describes is found in the pages of God's Word; rather, this kind of experience is condemned. As I read his description of meditation and Hemi-Sync, which is New Age and potentially demonic, it reminded me of the sober warning in Colossians 2:8-10.

> Don't let anyone capture you with empty philosophies and high-sounding nonsense that come from human thinking and from the spiritual powers of this world, rather than from Christ. For in Christ lives all the fullness of God in a human body. So you also are complete through your union with Christ, who is the head over every ruler and authority.

Universalism

Another disturbing aspect of Alexander's book is his claim of traveling to heaven without faith in Jesus Christ. He embraces an unbiblical viewpoint known as universalism, which teaches that everyone goes to heaven regardless of belief in Christ or even in spite of unbelief. He claims he went to heaven without faith in Jesus Christ and believes everyone else will go there too. Describing himself, he says,

> Although I considered myself a faithful Christian, I was so more in name than in actual belief. I didn't begrudge those who wanted to believe that Jesus was more than simply a good man who had suffered at the hands of the world. I sympathized deeply with those who wanted to believe that there was a God somewhere out there who loved us unconditionally. In fact, I envied such people the security that those beliefs no doubt provided. But as a scientist, I simply knew better than to believe them myself.[31]

Concerning everyone else, he says, "My experience showed me that the death of the body and the brain are not the end of consciousness, that human experience continues beyond the grave. More important, it continues under the gaze of a God who loves and cares about each one of us and about where the universe itself and all the beings within it are ultimately going."[32] Alexander believes "God is present in us at all times."[33]

Over and over again Alexander highlights the feeling of love and acceptance he experienced in the place he allegedly visited, that he had nothing to fear, and that there are many universes, with "love . . . at the center of them all."[34] What message could possibly be more appealing to our modern culture than that God loves you no matter what you do, that he accepts you as you are, and that nothing can tear you away from him? The central message Alexander brought back from heaven to share with the world runs like this:

> *You are loved and cherished.*
> You have nothing to fear.
> There is nothing you can do wrong.
> If I had to boil this entire message down to one sentence, it would run this way:
> *You are loved.*
> And if I had to boil it down further, to just one word, it would (of course) be, simply:
> *Love.*
> Love is, without a doubt, the basis of everything.[35]

The truth of God's Word is that those who reject God's gracious offer of salvation *do* have something to fear—God's eternal judgment (see Revelation 11:18; 20:11-15). According to Scripture, heaven is not where all beings are ultimately going. Hell is also real. Jesus himself made this abundantly clear: "You can enter God's Kingdom only through the narrow gate. The highway to hell is broad, and its gate is wide for the many who choose that way. But the gateway to life is very narrow and the road is difficult, and only a few ever find it" (Matthew 7:13-14). Jesus is the narrow gate that leads to eternal life, forgiveness, and heaven (see John 10:9). Jesus is the only Mediator, or go-between, connecting a holy God and sinful men and women (see 1 Timothy 2:5-6). No one will enter heaven without him (see John 3:3, 16).

One of the most enlightening and heartbreaking narratives in *Proof of Heaven* unfolds in December 2008 when Alexander makes his first visit back to church after his illness. His visit to church aroused strong memories of his trip to heaven. The climax of his visit is taking Communion: "At last, I understood what religion was really all about. Or at least was supposed to be about. I didn't just believe in God; I knew God. As I hobbled to the altar to take Communion, tears streamed down my cheeks."[36]

I was stunned by these words. Here's a man who claims to have visited heaven, taking the Lord's Supper or Communion for the first time after his alleged round-trip to heaven. He's participating in the most sacred act of the Christian faith yet making no mention of what Communion is all about. Alexander is thinking the Core, not the Christ. When Jesus instituted the Lord's Supper on the night before his death on the cross, Scripture tells us,

> Jesus took some bread and blessed it. Then he broke
> it in pieces and gave it to the disciples, saying, "Take
> this and eat it, for this is my body." And he took a

cup of wine and gave thanks to God for it. He gave it
to them and said, "Each of you drink from it, for this
is my blood, which confirms the covenant between
God and his people. It is poured out as a sacrifice to
forgive the sins of many." (Matthew 26:26-28)

That's what "religion" is all about—knowing God through
the substitutionary death and resurrection of Jesus Christ.
He died for me—in my place—for the forgiveness of sins.
The Lord's Supper is a memorial of Christ's once-for-all sacrifice for sin—his taking the judgment we deserve as he died
on the cross. Tragically, Alexander missed what it's all about
at the most opportune moment as he approached the sacred
precincts of the Communion altar.

As further evidence of his universalist beliefs, Alexander
has established a nonprofit, publicly supported charity called
Eternea. The purpose of Eternea is to serve as a repository
for all manner of "spiritually transformative experiences."[37] If
Alexander really ventured into the afterlife, he would know
the one requirement for entrance into heaven, namely, faith
in Jesus Christ as Savior and Lord (see Acts 4:12; Romans
5:1), and he would be telling everyone about it instead of
supporting vague notions of "spiritually transformative experiences." If he had really gone to heaven, he would know that
Jesus, the Lamb of God who takes away the sin of the world,
is the centerpiece of heaven (see Revelation 5:6). Every creature in heaven knows who Jesus is and what he has done.
They sing this song to Jesus in heaven:

You are worthy to take the scroll and break its seals and open it. For you were slaughtered, and your blood has ransomed people for God from every tribe and language and people and nation. And you have caused them to become a Kingdom of priests for our God. And they will reign on the earth. (Revelation 5:9-10)

How could Alexander have really traveled to heaven and not know the truth about Jesus as the one way to truth and life (see John 14:6)? The answer—he didn't go to heaven.

By his own admission, Alexander is now open to all kinds of spiritual experiences, tragically leading people away from heaven and God. My prayer is that he and those who read his book can find the truth in Jesus Christ before it's too late.

CHAPTER 6

HEAVEN IS FOR REAL—
IS IT FOR REAL?

I looked at him, kneeling in the kitchen chair with his towel-cape still tied
  around his neck. "Colton, you said you were in heaven and you did all
  these things . . . a lot of things. How long were you gone?"
My little boy looked me right in the eye and didn't hesitate. "Three
  minutes," he said. Then he hopped down from the chair and skipped
  off to play.

TODD BURPO

OF ALL THE new genre of heaven-and-back books, *Heaven Is for Real* is by far the most familiar to people. Released in 2010, the book has enjoyed stratospheric sales, selling close to ten million copies. Television morning shows and the Internet were abuzz with talks and interviews about the book. *Heaven Is for Real* has become standard reading for people who want to know what heaven is like. The view that many people today have of heaven is from this book.

In 2011, *Heaven Is for Real for Kids: A Little Boy's Astounding Story of His Trip to Heaven and Back* was published. A major motion picture based on the book was released by Sony Pictures in Spring 2014. It earned a whopping $91.3 million in US theaters. When the movie was released for home video sales in July 2014, it debuted at number one on "both the Nielsen VideoScan First Alert chart, which tracks overall disc sales, Blu-ray Disc and DVD combined, and Nielsen's dedicated Blu-ray Disc sales chart."[1] When it comes to sales, popularity, and exposure, *Heaven Is for Real* is definitely for real.

The story about young Colton Burpo and his brush with death and full recovery is a great human interest story, but the hook for the story is his claim of traveling to heaven and back. Colton's age at the time of his alleged trip—three years and ten months—is another captivating feature of the story. The majority of the response to the book is glowingly positive. Endorsements fill the first two pages of the book, extolling its message of hope, encouragement, and comfort.

But not all the feedback has been affirming. The reviews are mixed. Some have questioned the specific material in the book as well as the reliability of near-death experiences (NDEs) in general to provide information about life after death. I've read chapters in books and blog posts and watched YouTube videos critiquing *Heaven Is for Real*. The Southern Baptist Convention passed a resolution at its June 2014 convention in Baltimore criticizing so-called "heaven books," including *Heaven Is for Real*. Southern Baptist delegates to the convention focused on "the sufficiency of Scripture regarding the afterlife," cautioning against putting books about personal heaven experiences on the same level as the Bible's description of the afterlife. The resolution stated,

MARK HITCHCOCK || 93

"Many of these books and movies have sought to describe heaven from a subjective, experiential source, mainly via personal testimonies that cannot be corroborated." The resolution continued that because "the doctrines of the afterlife are critical to a full understanding of salvation and repentance," Southern Baptists "reaffirm the sufficiency of biblical revelation over subjective experiential explanations to guide one's understanding of the truth about heaven and hell."[2] A motion was offered by one of the delegates for *Heaven Is for Real* to be removed from LifeWay's shelves for theological reasons, but that request was ruled out of order.

I have to admit that critiquing the experience of a child is not easy or enjoyable, especially when the experience arises from a harrowing ordeal for him and his family. However, letting unbiblical claims stand without objection would be even worse. Paul Mathenia, a lifelong Baptist pastor who now leads an Arkansas-based ministry, wrote in a *Baptist Press* column that "the cuteness, innocence and honesty of 4-year-olds" must "bow before the divine revelation of God's Word."[3] I agree. Speaking of the movie, Mathenia says,

> On the one hand I am happy the movie is coming out. What a great opportunity to get people talking about heaven! Those who view the movie will be open to discussing its views of heaven compared to biblical teachings. A clear and accurate presentation of the Gospel can easily flow from this. . . . On the other hand I am saddened. Many people will

succumb to the real temptation to base their view of heaven on the word of a 4-year-old boy instead of the Word of God. This type of reaction has already followed the book.[4]

With the staggering popularity of *Heaven Is for Real* and the gravity of the issues involved, my simple purpose, as with the other heaven-and-back books, is to measure the claims and content of this book against our only infallible guide about heaven and life after death—the Bible.

A Matter of Life and Death

In February 2003, Colton Burpo, who was three years and ten months old, was misdiagnosed with the stomach flu when he was suffering acute appendicitis that eventually ruptured his appendix, coursing deadly poison through his veins. His parents, fearing something much worse than the stomach flu, wisely took him to another hospital, where he was correctly diagnosed and underwent emergency surgery. During his surgery for the ruptured appendix, he "almost died." No detailed statement from doctors about his NDE is included in the book, but there is no doubt he was gravely ill and near death.

About four months after his surgery and subsequent hospital stay, while riding in the car, young Colton told his parents that when he was near death, he "'went up out of' his body, that he had spoken with angels, and had sat in Jesus' lap."[5] He claims he was gone for three minutes.[6] After this initial revelation to his parents, Colton divulged information about his trip to heaven in piecemeal fashion over an extended period of time. Every new revelation by Colton in the book elicits awe and reinforcement from his parents. (His father, Todd Burpo, serves as pastor of Crossroads Wesleyan Church in Imperial, Nebraska.)

The way Todd Burpo knew what his son was telling him wasn't made up "was that he was able to tell us what we were doing in another part of the hospital."[7] Colton said to his father, "You were in a little room by yourself praying, and Mommy was in a different room and she was praying and talking on the phone."[8] Colton's knowledge when he was in dire condition is the primary proof used to validate the reality of Colton's trip to heaven.

While I don't know all the details, I do know that this conversation occurred four months after Colton's time in the hospital. It seems to me that at some point during the four months, he could have heard his parents discussing where they were while he was in surgery, or he could have heard his father telling someone else about it. It is my view that we must be careful not to invest this event with supernatural significance without considering other plausible explanations.

Furthermore, according to Colton, his array of experiences in heaven happened in three minutes. That seems problematic to me. Of course, some might say that heaven is timeless and one can accomplish a great deal there in three minutes. But Colton claims he sat in Jesus' lap, met John the

Baptist, saw all kinds of animals and people, met his grandfather, did homework, was taught by Jesus, met his sister, saw God's throne "a bunch of times,"[9] sat by the Holy Spirit, and witnessed the climactic Battle of Armageddon. All of this in three minutes. This stretches the limits of credulity.

But regardless of my skepticism about other details, the ultimate test of Colton's alleged trip to heaven is not his knowledge of what was happening in the hospital or whether his experience lasted only three minutes; it is whether the facts line up with God's Word. Does his experience square with Scripture? That's the final criterion, and that's what I will explore in this chapter.

Jesus and John the Baptist

Much of *Heaven Is for Real* is a narrative of question-and-answer sessions between Todd Burpo and his son Colton. As we examine the book, I want to give the context and content of those conversations and then provide the biblical counterbalance to these statements where applicable.

Tim Challies notes a repeated pattern in the conversations between Todd Burpo and his son: "Every one of Colton's experiences, or very nearly every one, follows a pattern. He tells his father some little detail. His father experiences a gasp or feels his heart skip a beat. 'I could hardly breathe. My mind was reeling. My head was spinning.' A Scripture verse comes to dad's mind that validates the experience. Colton gets bored and runs off. Repeat."[10] While that assessment may seem harsh, it does capture the essence of the ongoing interaction between Todd and Colton. Todd seems to swallow everything his son says with unhesitating credulity. He hangs on Colton's every word and stands ready to receive more instruction about heaven from his son. I point this out not to nitpick but simply to put the information in its proper context.

Early in the process of relating what he saw in heaven, Colton says to his father, "Did you know that Jesus has a cousin? Jesus told me his cousin baptized him." Todd then writes, "Just as I was processing the implications of my son's statement—that he had *met* John the Baptist—Colton spied a plastic horse among his toys and held it up for me to look at. 'Hey, Dad, did you know Jesus has a horse?' 'A horse?' 'Yeah, a rainbow horse. I got to pet him. There's lots of colors.'"[11] Todd is astounded by these statements, in spite of the fact that Revelation 19:11 says that when Jesus comes, he will ride a *white* horse, not a rainbow horse.

Describing Jesus, Colton says, "He has brown hair and he has hair on his face. . . . And his eyes . . . oh, Dad, his eyes are so pretty!"[12] In Revelation 1:12-20, the apostle John, the closest disciple to Jesus, sees the radiant, resurrected Christ and describes his penetrating eyes as "flames of fire," not as "pretty." Regarding these and other descriptions, John MacArthur says, "Many of the things Todd Burpo interprets as irrefutable proof his son was given special revelation are clearly little more than standard Sunday school stories with a typical preschooler's slightly distorted slant."[13]

The Red Markers

One fascinating back-and-forth between father and son occurs when Colton tells his father, "Jesus has red markers on him." Todd Burpo then writes,

> At that moment, my throat nearly closed with tears as I suddenly understood what Colton was trying to say. Quietly, carefully, I said, "Colton, where are Jesus' markers?" Without hesitation, he stood to his feet. He held out his right hand, palm up and pointed to the center of it with his left. Then he held out his left palm and pointed with his right hand. Finally, Colton bent over and pointed to the tops of both his feet. "That's where Jesus' markers are, Daddy," he said. I drew in a sharp breath. He saw this. He had to have. We know where the nails were driven when Jesus was crucified, but you don't spend a lot of time going over those gruesome facts with toddlers and preschoolers.[14]

Todd views this as ironclad validation that his son actually saw Jesus. However, I'm not so certain this is as straightforward as Todd makes it.

I consider my wife, for example, who has worked with preschool children at our church for about twenty years. She told me that many of the Bible storybooks she uses show Jesus with nail prints in his hands and feet and that most of the children in her classes know this. Pastor Burpo admits that he read many Bible stories to Colton from a Bible story-book.[15] Colton certainly could have seen this depiction of Jesus in one of the storybooks. Based on her experience with children, my wife doesn't see this knowledge on Colton's part as anything out of the ordinary for a child who has grown up in Sunday school. While my wife's experience is obviously anecdotal evidence, it does come from many years of involvement with children about Colton's age.

The real problem with Colton's description of the wounds of the Savior is that in a Roman crucifixion the nails were not driven into the palms of the hands but into the wrists between the carpals and the radius. The soft tissue in the hands could tear loose with the weight of the body. The notion that the nails were driven into the palms comes from John 20:20, 24-27:

> As he spoke, he showed them the wounds in his *hands* and his side. They were filled with joy when they saw the Lord! . . . One of the twelve disciples, Thomas (nicknamed the Twin), was not with the others when Jesus came. They told him, "We have seen the Lord!" But he replied, "I won't believe it unless I see the nail wounds in his *hands*, put my fingers into them, and place my hand into the wound in his side." Eight days later the disciples were together again, and this time Thomas was with them. The doors were locked; but suddenly,

as before, Jesus was standing among them. "Peace
be with you," he said. Then he said to Thomas, "Put
your finger here, and look at my *hands*. Put your
hand into the wound in my side. Don't be faithless
any longer. Believe!" (emphasis mine)

In these verses, the word *hands* occurs three times. The
English word *hands* gives the impression that the spikes were
driven through the palms of the hands. This is the common understanding, but it's not correct. Renowned New
Testament scholar D. A. Carson notes, "When the Romans
crucified someone, they either tied or nailed the victim
to the cross. If the latter, they drove the nails through his
wrists; the hands would not have supported the weight. But
both the Hebrew word for hand (*yad*) and the Greek word
(*cheir*) can include the wrist and forearm."[16] Hearing Colton's
description of the "red markers" in Jesus' palms, Todd Burpo
says, "We know where the nails were driven when Jesus was
crucified."[17] But upon further investigation, it appears he
doesn't know. Colton's description of the location of the nail
prints in Jesus' palms matches the common understanding
pictured in many Bible storybooks but does not fit what we
know of Roman crucifixion and the wounds of our Savior.

More "Proof"

Another of the revelations that stunned Todd and his wife,
Sonja, was Colton's description of his sister who died in his

mother's "tummy." Colton's mother had experienced a mis-
carriage two months into her pregnancy. Colton maintains
that he met his sister in heaven and that "God adopted her."[18]
Todd claims there was no way Colton could have known this
and that this proves his trip to heaven was real. However, he
then admits that he and his wife had previously told Colton's
older sister Cassie about it.[19]

It seems to me that Cassie could have told Colton about
this or that he could have overheard his parents talking about
it at some point. I have two sons and one grandson, and I
know they hear a lot more than I often realize. Nevertheless,
this is not proof of the reality of his claims, especially in light
of the conflicts and contradictions between his story and the
Bible. We have to weigh the entire book as a whole. Just
because we can't explain one or two details does not mean we
are required to accept everything in the book as fact.[20]

Heaven, Homework, and the Holy Spirit

Colton's story is filled with an assortment of details. Among
other things, Colton claims that he did homework in heaven,
that Jesus was his teacher, that there are lots of kids in heaven,
and that everyone has wings and flies except Jesus.[21]

Colton describes Jesus as sitting at the right hand of God
in heaven, which is biblically accurate, but adds, with his
father's prompting and questioning, that the angel Gabriel
sits at the left hand of the Father's throne.[22] This extrabiblical
information is interesting in light of Hebrews 1:13-14, where

Jesus, who is sitting at God's right hand, is contrasted with angels, who are sent out to minister to God's people. Jesus is *sitting*. Angels, including Gabriel, are *sent out*. There's nothing in God's Word to indicate that any angel is seated anywhere, not to mention at God's left hand.[23]

Colton claims to have "sat by God the Holy Spirit" and describes him as "kind of blue."[24] In the book of Revelation, the Holy Spirit is constantly called the "seven spirits of God" when the heavenly perspective is in view. This does not mean there are seven spirits but refers to the fullness or plentitude of the Spirit's power (seven is the biblical number of completion or perfection). Isaiah 11:1-2 and Zechariah 4:2 may be the Old Testament background for the seven spirits of God. In any event, the color blue in association with the Holy Spirit is foreign to God's Word.

Referring to the gates of heaven, Colton says, they "were made of gold and there were pearls on them."[25] Revelation 21:21 says, "The twelve gates were made of pearls—each gate from a single pearl!" Colton's description of the gates of glory is at odds with the apostle John's. He also claims to have seen Satan in heaven but refused to tell his father what he looked like. Weighing these descriptions, we can safely conclude that some of them contradict Scripture, others are inconsistent with it, and others can't be confirmed one way or the other. But in every case the things Colton shares go beyond the biblical revelations about heaven. For that reason, we shouldn't give them any credence.

What Does Jesus Look Like?

Throughout the book, Todd persistently asks Colton what Jesus looks like and frequently shows him pictures to see if they bear any resemblance.

> When Colton saw Jesus in heaven, what did he look like? The reason for the frequency of this particular topic was that as a pastor, I wound up spending a lot of time at hospitals, in Christian bookstores, and at other churches—all places where there are lots of drawings and paintings of Christ. Often, Sonja and the kids were with me, so it became sort of a game. When we came across a picture of Jesus, we'd ask Colton, "What about this one? Is that what Jesus looks like?"
>
> Invariably, Colton would peer for a moment at the picture and shake his tiny head. "No, the hair's not right," he would say. Or, "The clothes aren't right."
>
> This would happen dozens of times over the next three years.[26]

Todd's incessant curiosity about the physical appearance of Jesus is perplexing. We're never told in Scripture what Jesus looked like, nor are we ever encouraged to seek any information about his physical characteristics. If it were important for us to know, I assume God would have told us. Nevertheless, one evening in early 2007 Todd was at home checking e-mails and ran across a CNN report about a young Lithuanian American girl named Akiane Kramarik, who began having visions of heaven at age four. She began to paint at an early age, and one of her works was a portrait of Jesus titled *Prince of Peace*. (The sketch is included in *Heaven Is for Real*.) After seeing the portrait, Todd quickly calls Colton to look at the sketch.

> "Take a look at this," I said, nodding toward the computer monitor. "What's wrong with this one?"
>
> He turned to the screen and for a long moment said nothing.
>
> "Colton?"
>
> But he just stood there, studying. I couldn't read his expression.
>
> "What's wrong with this one, Colton?" I said again.
> Utter silence.
>
> I nudged him in the arm. "Colton?"
>
> My seven-year-old turned to look at me and said, "Dad, that one's right."
>
> Knowing how many pictures Colton had rejected, Sonja and I finally felt that in Akiane's portrait, we'd seen the face of Jesus. Or at least a startling likeness."[27]

The problem is that, while we don't know much about what Jesus looks like, it does seem to strain believability concerning what we do know. The picture looks little like a Hebrew man from the land of Israel with the pedigree of Jesus recorded in Matthew 1. Describing the Akiane portrait, Douglas Jacoby says, "Jesus has light eyes and streaks in his hair, which appears to be permed. He looks little like a Middle Easterner—more like a white American."[28]

Body Up

Colton also claims that he met his grandfather, "Pop," in heaven and describes him as having really big wings and wearing white clothing with a blue sash.[29] His grandfather died at age sixty-one in a car accident but appeared like a twenty-nine-year-old in heaven.[30]

Concerning his deceased grandfather, Colton Burpo says, "He's got a new body. Jesus told me if you don't go to heaven, you don't get a new body."[31] I believe both of these statements are incorrect in light of Scripture. Presently, believers who have died and gone to heaven are disembodied spirits, or "naked," using the apostle Paul's image:

> We know that when this earthly tent we live in is taken down (that is, when we die and leave this earthly body), we will have a house in heaven, an eternal body made for us by God himself and not by human hands. We grow weary in our present bodies, and we long to put on our heavenly bodies like new clothing. For we will put on heavenly bodies; we will not be spirits without bodies. (2 Corinthians 5:1-3)

The new glorified body will be resurrected when the Lord comes (see 1 Corinthians 15:35-55; 1 Thessalonians 4:16).

Three New Testament passages are used by some to support the view that deceased believers have a temporary body in heaven now as they await the Lord's coming. First, in Luke 16:19-31, both the rich man and Lazarus have some kind of bodily form immediately after they die. The rich man refers to Lazarus dipping his finger in some water and placing it on his burning tongue. While this could be used to teach the existence of temporary bodies, we need to be careful since the point of this passage is not to teach about bodies in heaven and hell, but rather about the torment of the rich man in hell.

Second, at the Transfiguration of Jesus in Matthew 17:1-3, Moses and Elijah appeared with Jesus in bodily form. So it seems they had some kind of temporary bodily existence. However, it's likely that in this special instance God gave Moses and Elijah bodies so they could appear to the disciples visibly with Jesus. However, all this proves for sure is that they had a body for this one, unique event in the life of Jesus. It doesn't prove that all believers have temporary bodies for the full duration of the intermediate state.

Third, Revelation 6:9-11 records a heavenly vision of the apostle John who sees the souls of some believers who are martyred for their faith in Christ.

> When the Lamb broke the fifth seal, I saw under
> the altar the souls of all who had been martyred
> for the word of God and for being faithful in their

testimony. They shouted to the Lord and said, "O
Sovereign Lord, holy and true, how long before
you judge the people who belong to this world and
avenge our blood for what they have done to us?"
Then a white robe was given to each of them. And
they were told to rest a little longer until the full
number of their brothers and sisters—their fellow
servants of Jesus who were to be martyred—had
joined them.

Since John sees these souls and they wear white robes, this
could be evidence for some kind of temporary body for believers in heaven before the resurrection. Randy Alcorn seems to
hold that view: "The martyrs' wearing white robes suggests
the possibility of actual physical forms, because disembodied
spirits presumably don't wear robes. The robes may well have
symbolic meaning, but it doesn't mean they couldn't also be
physical. The martyrs appear to have physical forms that John
could actually see."[32] While this interpretation is possible, the
bodies of these believers are not resurrected until Revelation
20:5. For me, the idea of a temporary body is negated by the
clear teaching of 2 Corinthians 5:1-5. During the interval
between one's death and the future resurrection of the eternal
body at the Rapture, there is no temporary body, but disembodied existence. Believers in heaven right now exist in
a bodiless state. Colton's statements about seeing his grandfather don't appear to line up with the biblical evidence.

Colton's statement "If you don't go to heaven, you

don't get a new body" is also inconsistent with Scripture. Unbelievers who don't go to heaven will come to life and experience a resurrection of the body according to Revelation 20:5. Jesus said there is a resurrection of the just and unjust (see John 5:29; see also Acts 24:15). Those who don't go to heaven will receive a new resurrected body. Of course, their resurrection body will be vastly different in quality from the glorified body of a believer. Nevertheless, they will live for eternity in hell in a corporeal or bodily form. Again, *Heaven Is for Real* misrepresents the biblical teaching about heaven.

The Battle of Armageddon

Near the end of the book, Colton highlights a coming war. He says, "There's going to be a war, and it's going to destroy this world. Jesus and the angels and the good people are going to fight against Satan and the monsters and the bad people. I saw it. . . . In heaven, the women and the children got to stand back and watch. So I stood back and watched. . . . But the men, they had to fight. And Dad, I watched you. You have to fight too. . . . You either get a sword or a bow and arrow, but I don't remember which. . . . Jesus wins. He throws Satan into hell. I saw it."[33]

His father interprets this as a reference to the Battle of Armageddon and proof that he was going to fight in it.[34] According to Colton's own words, not only did he see present events and people in heaven, he was permitted, like the apostle John, to see the final great war of the end times (see Revelation

16:16; 19:11-21). Yet Colton's depiction of the Armageddon War differs significantly from the biblical account.

According to Revelation, all the armies of the earth will assemble at Armageddon in the northern part of Israel (see Revelation 16:12-16). Armageddon, which means the hill or mountain of Megiddo, overlooks the expansive Jezreel Valley that is twenty miles long and fourteen miles wide. Napoleon called it the world's perfect battlefield. The armies muster there for a final great death struggle, and when Jesus appears in the heavens for his second coming, the armies turn their focus and fury against him. Revelation 19:19-21 describes his conquest and the climax of the Battle of Armageddon:

> I [John] saw the beast and the kings of the world and their armies gathered together to fight against the one sitting on the horse and his army. And the beast was captured, and with him the false prophet who did mighty miracles on behalf of the beast—miracles that deceived all who had accepted the mark of the beast and who worshiped his statue. Both the beast and his false prophet were thrown alive into the fiery lake of burning sulfur. Their entire army was killed by the sharp sword that came from the mouth of the one riding the white horse. And the vultures all gorged themselves on the dead bodies.

Amazingly, no military struggle or battle of any kind is recorded in Revelation 19. Jesus will defeat the amassed armies without any effort (see Psalm 2:9). As Dr. J. Dwight Pentecost once said in one of my classes at Dallas Theological Seminary, "All Jesus will have to do to completely vanquish his enemies is speak the words 'Drop dead!' and it will all be over." Jesus will slay his enemies with the sword that comes out of his mouth, which pictures his piercing, penetrating word. As 2 Thessalonians 2:8 says, "The Lord Jesus will kill [the Antichrist] with the breath of his mouth and destroy him by the splendor of his coming."

Colton's description of men with swords and arrows fighting in the Battle of Armageddon contradicts the Word of God. Describing the victory at Armageddon, John Phillips says, "There will be no war at all, in the sense that we think of war. There will be just a word spoken from Him who sits astride the great white horse. . . . Now He speaks a word, and the war is over."[35]

Our revelation about the future in general and the final great war of the ages in particular must come from God's Word, not alleged heavenly visits that contradict it. And we already know from God's final word in Revelation that Jesus wins. We don't need information from a trip to heaven to tell us that. Revelation 19–20 tells us that as clearly as language can.

Not for Real

As you can tell from my review to this point, I don't put any stock in *Heaven Is for Real* as an accurate guide to heaven or the afterlife. When viewed in light of God's Word, *Heaven*

Is for Real quickly begins to unravel. The foundation cracks and crumbles under the weight of scrutiny. I agree with this conclusion by Douglas Jacoby: "The theology of *Heaven Is for Real* reads as though it has been taken out of a children's Sunday school workbook. A nearly four-year-old would have heard a great deal of talk about God and the Bible. . . . Although it's certainly a fascinating story, in so many places it feels hokey. . . . I am afraid the account does not impress me as celestial. Whatever little Colton experienced, it was not a visit to heaven."[36]

If I'm correct, the question remains: What *did* happen to Colton Burpo? What did he see? Did he go someplace? I can't answer those questions. I can only say what did *not* happen to him. He did *not* go to heaven or see John the Baptist, Jesus, the Holy Spirit, or the Battle of Armageddon. How can I be sure? Because many of his depictions of people and events in heaven and the future contradict the descriptions of heaven and the end times given to us in the inspired, inerrant Word of God. How many contradictions does it take for Colton's experience to be legitimately called into question, invalidated, and ultimately rejected? We must have some final authority to judge experience by, and I believe that final authority is the Bible. Human experience must always bow to the Bible. No experience, no matter how comforting or carefully packaged, takes precedence over the inspired Word of God. As the prophet Isaiah said, "Look to God's instructions and teachings! People who contradict his word are completely in the dark" (Isaiah 8:20). As I have demonstrated, *Heaven Is for Real* contradicts the Bible in many places.

I know that Todd and Colton have responded in a general way to much of the criticism of their book, but I would like to see them respond to the specific issues I've raised here as well as those raised by many others. They have summarily dismissed the criticism leveled against them as mean or "awful," but that is not a reasoned response. They owe it to their readers and to God's people to answer the objections. If they cannot, then they need to come clean and renounce the contents of their book. One cannot write a book that makes such extraordinary claims and then dodge the facts simply by attributing bad motives to the critics. Nothing in my assessment of *Heaven Is for Real* is mean spirited or coming from a heart of jealousy or anger. I have simply attempted to measure their book by *the* Book. Some kind of explanation by the Burpos is required. No one is above criticism, including them—and me.

Heaven 2.0

Before we move on, I want to emphasize the one main problem with *Heaven Is for Real* that rises above the rest. Simply stated, the book undermines the sufficiency of God's Word about heaven. John MacArthur observes,

> One of the most troubling aspects of *Heaven Is for Real* is the way Todd Burpo constantly

insinuates that personal experiences—even the
spectral memories of a three-year-old boy under
anesthetics—are somehow more compelling
than Scripture alone. "I had been a Christian
since childhood and a pastor for half my life, so I
believed that before. But now I *knew* it." Colton's
experiential exegesis of heaven has clearly made a
far more profound impact on Todd (and has been
more formative in his notion of the afterlife) than
anything he had previously gleaned about heaven
from his own study of Scripture.[37]

Tim Challies is also direct but right on in his analysis:

If you struggle believing what the Bible says, but
learn to find security in the testimony of a toddler,
well, I feel sorry for you. And I do not mean this in
a condescending way. If God's Word is not sufficient
for you, if the testimony of his Spirit, given to
believers, is not enough for you, you will not find
any true hope in the unproven tales of a child. This
hope may last for a moment, but it will not sustain
you, it will not bless you, in those times when hope
is waning and times are hard.[38]

The main thesis underlying *Heaven Is for Real*, and the
other heaven books, whether intentional or not, is that what
we have in the Bible is not enough. The revelation from the

holy prophets and apostles is insufficient, so we need an update—what we might call *Heaven 2.0.*

All the writers of these books claim that they were the recipients of this special revelation from God to convince them that heaven is real and to pass that message on to the rest of us. In other words, the Bible is not enough to convince them or us that heaven is real, yet ironically, they claim that their book is enough to convince us. If we will only read their book, we will know that heaven is real and it's a wonderful place. The logic here is circular. If someone doesn't or won't believe the Bible's revelation about heaven, why would he or she believe their story? The question is—whom do we believe? Is the Bible enough, or do we need something else?

Tim Challies summarizes the matter:

> When a Christian, or a person who claims to be a Christian, tells me that he has been to heaven, am I obliged to believe him or at least to give him the benefit of the doubt?
>
> No, I am under no such obligation. I do not believe that Don Piper or Colton Burpo or Mary Neal or Bill Wiese visited the afterlife. They can tell me all the stories they want, and they can tell those stories in a sincere tone, but I do not believe them. . . . I am not necessarily saying that these people are liars—just that I am under no *obligation* to believe another person's experience.[39]

This issue, along with many others, will be addressed in more detail in the next chapter as we expose and explain some of the basic, underlying problems that plague the entire genre of heavenly memoirs.

CHAPTER 7

TROUBLE IN PARADISE

One of the great attractions of these near-heaven experiences . . . is how
  utterly personal and loving the picture is. . . . To the plethora of
  burning questions most people ask—"Is there a God? Does he love me?
  Will I be reunited with the people I love? Will I ever know boundless
  joy? Is there life after death?"—the near-heaven narratives say, "Yes, yes,
  yes, yes, and yes!"

MARK GALLI

When an NDE clearly contradicts Scripture or orthodox biblical
  scholarship, warning bells should begin to ring. We know that the Bible
  is true. We don't know that a particular report of an NDE is true, so
  the Bible must always take precedence over an NDE story regardless of
  how much we may want to believe it.

DOUGLAS JACOBY

I'VE TOUCHED ON many of the concerns with the recent rash
of heavenly memoirs briefly throughout this book, and up
to this point, I've been more detailed in my critique against
individual books. Here in this chapter, however, I want
to examine the books together. I want to pull the threads
together and put these books through a final examination.

In my estimation, five simple arguments against the
heaven-and-back books will suffice to show why they should
be avoided and even rejected by those who claim to be followers of Christ.

Four and No More

One argument against the authenticity of the heaven-and-back books is the sheer number of people claiming to have this experience in modern times compared to the very few people in Scripture who received visions of heaven. The number of people allegedly traveling to heaven in the last few years is staggering. Heaven has become a choice travel destination. Just in the last decade hundreds of people claim to have made the trip. And at least a few maintain they visited the bowels of hell. The claims are astounding. Think about it. In *23 Minutes in Hell* we have a professed believer in Christ in hell. In *Proof of Heaven* we have a confessed skeptic and unbeliever in heaven. And in *A Divine Revelation of Hell* and *A Divine Revelation of Heaven*, Mary Baxter, who professes to be a Christian, claims to have visited both places.

All these claims fall short when measured against God's Word. The Bible says people don't go to heaven and come back. Proverbs 30:4 asks the question "Who has ascended to heaven and come down?" (ESV). The answer in John 3:13 is definitive: "No one has ascended into heaven except he who descended from heaven, the Son of Man" (ESV). Only four people in all of biblical history went to heaven and came back, and none of them were near death at the time. Additionally, *no one* in all Scripture had a direct vision of hell or made a trip there and back.

The only people who ever really came back from a state of biological death are the select individuals in Scripture whom one of the Old Testament prophets or Jesus or his disciples raised from the dead. And as far as we know, none of them related any experiences about traveling to heaven or what they saw and heard. Lazarus was dead (not just near death) for four days and came back to life. Yet there's no evidence that he came back with tantalizing tales from the crypt. Even the apostle Paul, who was caught up to heaven on one occasion, did not reveal the things he saw there (see 2 Corinthians 12:1-5). Not only was Paul forbidden to give detailed information about his visit to heaven, but he was also given a thorn in the flesh to keep him from being overcome with pride due to his visit. The thorn was evidently some painful physical ailment. If the apostle Paul needed some physical malady to keep him humble after his visit to heaven, one would expect that anyone else would need the same preventive.

Only three people in the entire Bible—Ezekiel, Isaiah, and the apostle John—were given a vision of heaven and then permitted by God to tell us something of what it's like. Doesn't it seem strange that God would suddenly allow hundreds of people to enter the portals of heaven and return to tell about it?

To bolster the biblical support for near-death visits to heaven, some people point to the New Testament example of Stephen. In Acts 7 Stephen became the first martyr of Christianity when he was stoned to death in Jerusalem by the religious leaders for his faith in Jesus as Messiah and Lord. As he was pelted with stones, Stephen uttered these incredible words: "Behold, I see the heavens opened up and the Son of Man standing at the right hand of God" (Acts 7:56, NASB). Every other place the Bible mentions Jesus being at the Father's right hand, he is always seated. But here Jesus is standing. Why? To receive the first martyr of the church and to welcome his faithful servant to heaven. So, at least in this one case, we can say that sometimes God may give a person a glimpse of glory just before he or she dies. But there's an important distinction between a death-bed vision (DBV), also called a near-death vision, and a near-death experience (NDE). The main difference is that in the case of Stephen and others who have DBVs of heaven, they died immediately or very quickly after the vision. They see a brief vision of heaven and then go there, without any return to earth.

Another well-known story outside the Bible that affirms the possibility of DBVs for believers is the death of the famous evangelist D. L. Moody.[1] In August 1899 in New York City, four months before he died, Moody made this triumphant statement: "Someday you will read in the papers that Dwight Moody is dead. Don't you believe a word of it! At that moment I shall be more alive than I am now. . . . I was born of the flesh in 1837; I was born of the Spirit in 1855. That which is born of the flesh may die. That which is born of the Spirit shall live forever."

Four months later, on December 22, Moody lay dying. Early that morning his son Will was surprised to hear his father's voice from across the room. "Earth recedes, heaven opens before me!" Will quickly came over, and Moody said,

"This is no dream, Will. It is beautiful. . . . If this is death, it is sweet. There is no valley here. God is calling me and I must go. Don't call me back!" The great evangelist slipped back into what appeared to be unconsciousness. Moody awoke a few hours later to see his wife and family around him. He told his wife, "I went to the gate of heaven. Why, it is so wonderful." Within a few hours Moody drew his final breath of air on this earth.

Billy Graham similarly provides this moving account of his grandmother's death:

> When my maternal grandmother died, for instance, the room seemed to fill with a heavenly light. She sat up in bed and almost laughingly said, "I see Jesus. He has His arms outstretched toward me. I see Ben [her husband who had died some years earlier] and I see the angels." She slumped over, absent from the body but present with the Lord.[2]

What are we to make of such stories? Were the DBVs of Moody and Billy Graham's grandmother real or imagined? I guess there's no way to prove either way for sure. But we can say from Stephen's experience that this kind of thing has some biblical support. We know that it happened at least once in the Bible. Personally, I have no reason to doubt the reality of such accounts as long as they don't contain information that contradicts Scripture. Nevertheless, we need to remember that there's only one instance of a DBV in the Bible.

With this solitary occurrence, God may be trying to tell us not to expect these as common but also not to totally discount them all either. If God in his grace and mercy chooses to grant some of his children an early glimpse of glory just before death, as he did for Stephen, D. L. Moody, and Billy Graham's grandmother, we should accept it and thank him for it as another demonstration of his matchless grace. But these instances are very different from the detailed accounts of those who claim to visit heaven when near death and come back to tell the rest of us about it.

The Lamb and the Glory

A second major flaw in the heavenly memoirs is their consistent focus on the mundane instead of the majestic. Concerning almost all of these books, one can say, "There is little that points to the centrality of Jesus Christ in the scope of redemption. No mention is made of Christ's life, death, or resurrection in these accounts."[3] Revelation 5:6 tells us that the Lamb (Jesus) is in the center of everything in heaven, which teaches us a very important lesson—if Jesus is the center of heaven, how much more should he be the center of our lives, our homes, our marriages, and our churches? Yet in the heaven-and-back books, the most important thing about heaven is strangely absent. The central attraction is missing or at least minimized.

Revelation 21:11 and 21:23 emphasize that heaven is enveloped by the glory of God and illuminated like an infinite floodlight. But the heavenly memoirs for the most part deal with people they see, mansions, angels, flowers, and all kinds of details and information that everyone wants to hear. John MacArthur notes,

> We live in a narcissistic culture, and it shows in these accounts of people who claim they've been to heaven. They sound as if they viewed paradise in a mirror, keeping themselves in the foreground. They say comparatively little about God or His glory. But the glory of God is what the Bible says fills, illuminates, and defines heaven. Instead, the authors of these stories seem obsessed with details like how good they felt—how peaceful, how happy, how comforted they were; how they received privileges and accolades; how fun and enlightening their experience was; and how many things they think they now understand perfectly that could never be gleaned from Scripture alone. In short, they glorify self while barely noticing God's glory. They highlight everything but what's truly important about heaven.[4]

He concludes with this penetrating insight:

> It is quite true that heaven is a place of perfect bliss—devoid of all sorrow and sin, full of exultation and enjoyment—a place where grace and peace reign totally unchallenged. Heaven is where every

true treasure and every eternal reward is laid up for
the redeemed. Anyone whose destiny is heaven will
certainly experience more joy and honor there than
the fallen mind is capable of comprehending—
infinitely more than any fallen creature deserves. But
if you actually saw heaven and lived to tell about it,
those things are not what would capture your heart
and imagination. You would be preoccupied instead
with the majesty and grace of the One whose glory
fills the place.[5]

The absence of the Lamb and his glory in the heavenly
memoirs is inexplicable if the memoirs are real.

The Bible Tells Me So

For me, the most egregious error in the heavenly tourism books
is their penchant for going beyond—*far* beyond—Scripture.
I've addressed this problem throughout the book, but here I
want to drill down a bit deeper. Heaven-and-back books are
postscripts to the Bible's revelation about heaven in spite of
strong warnings in Scripture not to go beyond the revelation
God has given us about heaven or other areas of biblical truth.
First Corinthians 4:6 states the important principle that we are
"not to exceed what is written" (NASB) in God's Word.

Our most detailed source of information about heaven is
found in two places in the book of Revelation: chapters 4–5
and 21–22. God gave the apostle John this unique unveiling

of the future world and life there. But remember, after John received his vision of heaven, God added this serious warning: "I testify to everyone who hears the words of the prophecy of this book: if anyone adds to them, God will add to him the plagues which are written in this book; and if anyone takes away from the words of the book of this prophecy, God will take away his part from the tree of life and from the holy city, which are written in this book" (Revelation 22:18-19, NASB). These are some of the final words of God in the Bible. And last words are lasting words. The book of Revelation closed God's Word about heaven and the afterlife. We add to it at our own peril.

The underlying premise of all these books is that God's Word is incomplete or somehow ineffective to let us know that heaven and hell are real—that we need more than God has given us in the Bible. Without exception, the author of each book says that God wanted him or her to tell people about the experience so readers will know that heaven or hell is real. But don't we already know that if we read the Bible? All God wants us to know about heaven, hell, and the afterlife is found within the sixty-six books in the Bible. As Doug Groothuis says, "It is far better to trust the word of the One who has conquered death through his matchless resurrection than to rely on the reports of the resuscitated."[6]

Many will probably say that I'm overreacting—that these extrabiblical stories and speculations about heaven are helpful in some respects or at least harmless. But A. W. Tozer, in a chapter titled "There Is No Substitute for Theology," takes that view to task: "Whatever keeps me from my Bible is my enemy, however harmless it may appear to be. Whatever engages my attention when I should be meditating on God and things eternal does injury to my soul. . . . Let me accept anything else instead of the Scriptures and I have been cheated and robbed to my eternal confusion."[7]

Tozer goes on to say that every alleged spiritual experience must be measured by God's Word:

Whatever originates outside the Scriptures should for that very reason be suspect until it can be shown to be in accord with them. If it should be found to be contrary to the Word of revealed truth, no true Christian will accept it as being from God. However high the emotional content, no experience can be proved to be genuine unless we can find chapter and verse authority for it in the Scriptures. "To the word and to the testimony" must always be the last and final proof. Whatever is new or singular should also be viewed with a lot of caution until it can furnish scriptural proof of its validity.[8]

This is one of the glaring weaknesses of the heaven-and-back books. They are "high [on] emotional content," as Tozer says, and carry a sensational appeal that makes them very alluring and appealing to modern readers. However, they fail the biblical test. Most of these books are generously sprinkled with Bible verses, yet whenever they cite the Bible or quote it, they use it "only to *validate*, not *evaluate*" their experiences.[9] The heavenly tourism books are in some ways a troubling sign of the times. The explosion of these books unearths the trend in modern times to give the Bible a backseat to exciting spiritual or emotional experiences. Tim Challies writes,

> The very idea of God calling a person to heaven and back and then having that person share his experience in order to bolster our faith is the exact opposite of what the Lord desires for us. . . . Faith is believing that what God says in his Word is true and without error. You dishonor God if you choose to believe what the Bible says only when you receive some kind of outside verification. You dishonor God if you need this kind of outside verification.[10]

John Piper states, "If books go beyond Scripture, I doubt what they say about heaven. . . . I don't bother to read these books. Since I have my Bible, which already tells me what I can know for sure about heaven, and everything in those books I do not know for sure . . . it's all guesswork, and I don't find guesswork about heaven helpful, therefore I don't read the books."[11]

Piper even goes so far as to compare the near-heaven books with the forbidden practice of communicating with the dead. He claims that God's beef with consulting the dead is that it belittles God's revelation to man. We dishonor God when we seek information elsewhere. Piper explains his argument:

The Bible forbids séances and necromancy. That is,
it forbids communicating with the dead. Whether
or not you bring them up like the witch of Endor
brought up Samuel, or whether they happen to
show back up in your living room . . . I don't think
in principle there's any difference. . . . The argument
that God gives for why we shouldn't do it applies
to both. Here's what it is: Isaiah 8:19: "When
they say to you, 'Inquire of the mediums and the
necromancers who chirp and mutter,' should not a
people inquire of their God? Should they inquire of
the dead on behalf of the living?" In other words,
God's beef with necromancy is that it belittles the
sufficiency of his communication. "Why would you
inquire of the dead to find out what you want to
know instead of inquiring of me?" And if they say,
"Well, I have inquired of you and you didn't tell me
what I want to know," he would say, "Well, that's
your problem. I have told you what you need to
know. You don't need to know about such and such
if I haven't told you. And, in fact, if you go trying to
inquire about such and such that I haven't told you,
you are dishonoring me." So that's the nature of the
argument. And, therefore, I think the prohibition
of séances and necromancy applies to this kind
of thing and people ought to stop writing those
books.[12]

The bottom line is this: what's in Scripture is sure; what's in these books is suspect at best. Why not stick with the sure? There's plenty in these books to alert believers to stay far away.

I'm afraid some of these authors are trying to upstage the Bible with their sensational revelations. Nothing could be more dangerous. C. Michael Patton observes, "I have often said that left unchecked, experience is the most powerful and compelling source for theology. You can argue with logic, facts, evidence, and the like, but it is almost impossible to argue against subjective experience. However, if our experience comes in direct contradiction with correctly interpreted Scripture, Scripture should always win."[13] We call this the doctrine of *sola Scriptura*, which means that Scripture is our only final, infallible source of authority.

Of course, this does not totally discount experience. God can and does use experience to confirm the truth to his people. The apostle Paul, on one occasion, appeals to the experience of the Galatian believers concerning how they received the Holy Spirit, whether by faith or by works (see Galatians 3:2-5). Their experience lined up with God's Word. Valid experience always will. Experience can confirm the truth, but valid experience will never contradict Scripture.

Experience is wonderful, but only if it stands straight against the plumb line of God's Word. As David Platt wisely says, "Let's minimize the thoughts of man; magnify, trust, let's bank our lives and our understanding of the future on the truth of God."[14]

Angel of Light

As we've seen in our examination of some of the heaven-and-back books, much of the idle speculation that comes from NDEs sounds more occultic and New Age than biblical. The most common description of NDEs is seeing a beautiful, bright light. The Bible says that since God is light, Satan disguises himself as an angel of light to deceive the unsuspecting (see 2 Corinthians 11:14). Doesn't it make sense that the great deceiver would want people on earth to believe that one's relationship to Christ has no bearing on seeing the great light and entering heaven? This is Satan's greatest lie. We shouldn't be surprised that he would employ a powerful experience like an NDE to give some people false security about their eternal destiny. Please don't misunderstand me here. I'm *not* saying or even implying that all of the "I went to heaven" stories are demonically controlled counterfeits. But on the other hand, we would be foolish to totally discount the idea that some of them are. Satan traffics in deceit—and what ploy would be more effective than trips to paradise for all, regardless of one's relationship to God through Jesus Christ?

He Said, She Said

Throughout this book I've tried to point to specific instances where the books about heavenly visits are at odds with the Bible's descriptions of heaven and the afterlife. However, these books not only contradict the Bible, they consistently contradict one another. The heaven-and-back books contain many glaring discrepancies. The descriptions of heaven are all over the place. NDEs seem to possess a few common features in that most describe going through a dark tunnel, seeing a bright light, and so on. But that's where the similarities end.

I've read at least twenty of these books and scanned many, many more, and each one is a unique adventure. Not only do these books conflict with Scripture at key points; they also contradict one another, giving varying reports about the afterlife, which cannot all be true. William Alnor observes,

> In recent years I have examined many of the most popular "I went to heaven" stories circulating through the church. As a result of my inquiry I am throwing up a bright red flag of caution over believing *any* of the current heaven or hell visitation stories. We cannot trust them. The stories are confusing at times partly due to their mystical nature. But they are usually contradictory on significant details. Out of all the stories I've examined there were no perfect matches. In other words one man's picture of heaven did not correlate with the pictures given to us by any of the others.[15]

Some of the alleged visitors to heaven see other people such as deceased relatives or biblical characters like John the Baptist, whereas others see no people in heaven. In a more extreme case, Mary K. Baxter sees a room of tears, a room of records, and a storehouse of blessings. No other heaven books mention any of these or anything even remotely similar. These are but a few examples of the many contradictions that exist between these stories.

In stark contrast, the biblical accounts of heavenly visions in Ezekiel 1, Isaiah 6, and Revelation 4–5 and 21–22 bear a remarkable similarity to one another and little similarity to the modern heavenly memoirs. The vision God's Word gives us of heaven is thrilling and consistent.

I want to delve into these chapters in God's Word that tell us about heaven, but before we go there, I want to make one more brief stop to consider the flip side of the heavenly memoirs—purported visits to the halls of hell.

CHAPTER 8

TO HELL AND BACK

Hell is certainly out of fashion. In an age of "tolerance," it represents the ultimate intolerance. Hell, by its very definition, means someone is wrong and will suffer the consequences of his or her error.

DOUGLAS J. RUMFORD

I LIKE THE STORY of an Illinois man who left the snowballed streets of Chicago for a vacation in Florida. His wife was on a business trip and was planning to meet him there the next day. When he reached his hotel, he decided to send his wife a quick e-mail. Unable to find the scrap of paper on which he had written her e-mail address, he did his best to type it in from memory. Unfortunately, he missed one letter, and his note was directed instead to an elderly preacher's wife whose husband had passed away only the day before. When the grieving widow checked her e-mail, she saw this note on the screen:

Dearest Wife,

Just got checked in. Everything prepared for your arrival tomorrow.

Your Loving Husband.

P.S. Sure is hot down here.

We all get a good laugh out of that story and others like it, but many are claiming today that they have gone to hell and been sent back with a message for the rest of us. They've been sent back to tell us, "Sure is hot down here."

Let's face it: hell is a hot topic today. And hell is under fire. At the same time many are claiming to have visited hell and returned to warn us about it, there's a growing chorus of voices within evangelical Christianity that either denies the existence of hell (or at least that anyone will end up there) or decreases its duration (punishment in hell is not everlasting). What are we to make of all this?

I want to be clear at the outset that I believe hell is real, literal, and eternal. The Bible describes hell as a real place where the souls of the unredeemed will spend an eternity separated from God and his goodness (see 2 Thessalonians 1:9). Jesus tells a powerful parable (recorded in Luke 16:19-31) that graphically portrays hell as a literal place where an unrepentant rich man immediately goes when he dies. He is pictured as being conscious, having awareness of his surroundings, and fully remembering his life on earth. Jesus said there is no escape from the clutches of hell (see Luke 16:26) and that the punishment there is never ending (see Mark 9:43-48). There is no second chance at salvation. There are no do-overs. The old saying is true: "As death finds us, eternity keeps us."

Some people might be surprised to learn that eleven of the twelve times the word *gehenna* (hell) occurs in the New Testament, it is found on the lips of the Savior himself. Make no mistake: Jesus believed in a literal place called hell. He talked about it more than any other person in the Bible. In fact, Jesus talked about hell more than he talked about heaven.

In the well-known Sermon on the Mount (Matthew 5–7) Jesus refers to hell or final judgment at least six times. Just two days before he died on the cross, Jesus preached his great end-times sermon on the Mount of Olives. In that message, Jesus spoke of final judgment several times. The final sobering verse of this sermon says, "They [meaning the unrighteous] will go away into eternal punishment, but the righteous will go into eternal life" (Matthew 25:46). Jesus affirms the existence of both hell and heaven in one short sentence. Jesus is our major biblical source for the reality of a literal place called hell. As John Blanchard says, "To believe in heaven but not in hell is to declare that there were times when Jesus was telling the truth and times when he was lying."[1]

Hell is real—that much is clear from Scripture and the Savior—but what is hell like? Where do we turn to find out who goes there and what it's like?

As with heaven, we should get our information about hell from the Bible. Yet many today seem to believe the Bible isn't sufficient to unveil the underworld. Millions today are turning to alleged firsthand accounts of the horrors of hell to get the inside information. The authors of these books claim they've been to hell and back and want the rest of us to know that it's real and really bad.

We spent quite a bit of time examining the claims of the "I've been to heaven" books, and I believe it's important to spend at least one chapter briefly considering two of the best-selling "I've been to hell" books.

A Divine Revelation of Hell

If the title *A Divine Revelation of Hell* sounds familiar, it should. In chapter 3, we considered Mary K. Baxter's book *A Divine Revelation of Heaven*. Baxter claims she made a series of round-trips to both hell and heaven. She maintains that Jesus took her into hell for thirty nights in 1976.

Baxter's book is very graphic and detailed but is also quite repetitive. Baxter portrays hell as being in the shape or structure of a human body. She describes a left and right leg, a left and right arm, and jaws, with each section containing various torture chambers. She also describes the "Pits," "Belly," "Cells," and "Heart" of hell. She claims "hell is in the center of the earth."[2] Jesus tells her that in hell "the cells are seventeen miles high."[3]

Her descriptions are overly detailed in many places and appear contrived to me. Here's one example:

> Jesus told me that there is a place in hell called the
> "fun center." Souls confined to the pits cannot be

brought there. He also told me that though torments
are different for different souls, all are burned with
fire.

The fun center is shaped like a circus arena.
Several people who are to be the entertainment are
brought to the center ring of the fun center. These
are people who knowingly served Satan on earth.
They are the ones who, of their own free will, chose
to follow Satan instead of God. Around the sides
of the arena are the other souls, except those from
the pits.[4]

Baxter's book is filled with repeated accounts of souls
in hell suffering horrific torment at the hands of Satan and
demons. In story after story the people she sees in hell want
out and want a second chance.

The most startling part of the story is her account of
being left in hell alone and suffering torment and unspeak-
able anguish.

Jesus said, "Follow me." We walked up a flight of
stairs into the heart, where a doorway was opened
before us. In the heart was total darkness. I heard the
sounds of crying, and there was an odor so awful I
could barely breathe. All I could see in the darkness
was Jesus. I walked very close to Him.

And then, all of a sudden, Jesus was gone! The
unthinkable had happened. I was alone in the heart

of hell. Horror took hold of me. Fear gripped my soul, and death took hold of me.

I cried out to Jesus, "Where are You? Where are You? Oh, please come back, Lord!" I called and I called, but no one answered. . . . As we went deeper into the heart, I felt a horrible pain as some force rubbed my body. It seemed as though my very flesh was being ripped off me. I screamed out in terror. My captors dragged me to a cell and threw me inside. As they locked the door, I cried even louder. . . . Fear—the most awesome fear—gripped my soul.[5]

Baxter continues the harrowing narrative:

A feeling of intense loneliness and utter despair fell upon me. . . . I cried out into the darkness, "I do not belong here. I am saved. I belong to God. Why am I here?" But there was no answer. . . . Something unseen was tearing at my body, while evil spirits in the form of bats were biting me all over.[6]

Later, she alleges that Jesus abandoned her in hell a second time, where she was again attacked and tormented by demons. When she finally got out of hell, she was so afraid of going back there that she was fearful to even have Jesus near her sometimes.[7]

Baxter believes she saw visions of end-times events and

a prophecy from Jesus himself. She saw the Antichrist, the number 666—the mark of the Beast—and the return of Jesus Christ to earth.

23 Minutes in Hell

The other main hell-and-back book, *23 Minutes in Hell*, was written by Bill Wiese. It also hit the *New York Times* Best Sellers List. Wiese professes faith in Jesus Christ as his Savior. He says openly, "I was a Christian in hell."[8] His purported twenty-three minutes in hell occurred at 3:00 a.m. on Sunday, November 22, 1998, when he found himself "catapulted out of my bed into the very pit of hell."[9] According to Wiese, it was not a dream. He was literally in hell—a place where he says the heat was unbearable. Hell, he maintains, is a literal burning inferno—a pit one mile across—in the center of the earth.[10]

In hell he was immediately confronted by two towering beasts ten to thirteen feet tall that resembled reptiles who tortured him viciously. He heard screams of many other people wailing in torment. Demons grabbed him, crushed his head, and were about to pull his body apart at one point. Wiese says while he was in hell, "I didn't even possess the thought of calling on God for help, because I was there as one who didn't know God. The Lord didn't even come to mind."[11] This detail is strange to me. How can someone who claims to be a Christian experience a time when he or she doesn't know God?

He says the reason the Lord sent him to hell was so he could come back and tell the rest of us that hell is real. But if we believe the Bible, don't we already know that? Other than a bunch of gory, ghoulish details, what Wiese says is nothing new.

On a positive note, Wiese does clearly present the gospel message of salvation and forgiveness of sins through faith in Jesus Christ. I'm grateful for his clear expression of the gospel. I pray that some who read his book will come to faith in Christ in spite of the errors his book contains. One glaring example of error is his statement that during his time in hell, "[Jesus] removed the knowledge that I was a Christian."[12] Wiese is saying that Jesus actually took from him the knowledge that he even knew the Lord. God's Word is clear that the Lord wants his people to always enjoy full assurance of our relationship with him (see Hebrews 6:11). The one who sows seeds of doubt and unbelief in the hearts and minds of believers is Satan and his demonic host, not the Lord. Why would God ever remove from one of his children the knowledge that he or she is a Christian? This notion is totally foreign to Scripture.

Paradise Lost

The hell-and-back books are not as numerous as the heaven-and-back books, but they're just as fraught with error. The first major problem is that in both of the main hell-and-back books the person who spent considerable time in hell claims to be a Christian. Both Baxter and Wiese profess faith in Christ. Stop and think about this for a moment—a Christian in hell. This goes against every promise the Lord has made to his people.

Jesus said, "I will never fail you. I will never abandon you" (Hebrews 13:5). Yet Jesus supposedly abandoned Mary Baxter—and not in just any place, but in hell, and not just once, but twice. The Bible says that nothing can ever separate the believer from God's love (see Romans 8:38-39). Baxter insists that she suffered wrenching desperation when she was left alone in hell. Describing when she was alone in hell, she says,

> A fear like I had never felt before came on me. My flesh was again being torn from me, and a great chain was being wrapped around my body. I looked down at myself as the chain was placed on me. I looked like the others. I was a skeleton full of dead men's bones. Worms crawled inside of me, and a fire began at my feet and enveloped me in flames. . . . I was gripped by the most awful emotions. I could not feel God, nor love, nor peace, nor warmth. But I could feel with the keenest of senses, fear, hatred, excruciating pain and sorrow beyond measure. I called out to the Lord Jesus to save me, but there was no answer.[13]

Jesus promised his followers eternal protection from judgment and the evil one. The apostle John writes, "We know that God's children do not make a practice of sinning, for God's Son holds them securely, and the evil one cannot touch them" (1 John 5:18). If what Baxter describes in hell is true, then Jesus broke his solemn promise to her. But since Jesus is God and cannot lie, then it's Baxter who is either mistaken or not telling the truth.

Speak of the Devil

A second major flaw in these hell-and-back books is the depiction of hell teeming with demons and with Satan often present. Wiese says during his time in hell, demons grabbed him and tried to pull him apart. Yet the Bible says that Satan and demons aren't presently in hell. Satan and demons are *destined* for hell or the lake of fire (see Revelation 20:10), but they aren't there now. Understanding what the Bible says about the parts of the underworld helps clear up some confusion about the who, when, and where of hell. According to Scripture there are four words for parts of hell.

- *Gehenna*—This word is found twelve times in the New Testament and is derived from the Valley of Hinnom just west of the city of Jerusalem, which served as the city dump. Jesus, who spoke this word eleven of the twelve times it occurs in the New Testament, borrowed the vivid imagery of refuse, worms, maggots, and never-ending smoldering fires in using the word. Gehenna is the same place as "the fiery lake of burning sulfur" (Revelation 20:10), "the lake of fire" (Revelation 20:14), and "the second death," which refers to eternal separation from God (Revelation 20:6, 14). All unredeemed humans, all demons, and Satan will end up there, but none of them are there now. Presently, Gehenna is uninhabited.

- *Hades*—Found ten times in the New Testament, the Greek word *hades* can be a synonym for the grave (see Acts 2:27, 31), but the majority of occurrences refer to the place where the souls of lost people are presently confined while they await the final day of judgment. Hades is like the county jail where inmates are held until their trial and their transfer to the penitentiary (Gehenna), where they will serve out their eternal sentence.

- *The Abyss*—The shaft of the abyss is the present place of confinement for some demons who go too far in their rebellion against God (see Luke 8:31). These demons in the abyss will be released for five months in the end times during the Tribulation to mercilessly afflict unbelievers on earth (see Revelation 9:1-9).

- *Tartarus*—Mentioned only once in the New Testament in 2 Peter 2:4, Tartarus is the prison house for fallen angels (demons) who sinned heinously in Genesis 6:1-4 by cohabiting with women. In Greek mythology, Tartarus was the lowest chamber of the underworld. The demons locked there will remain

in custody until the day of their final judgment (see
2 Peter 2:4).

As we can see from these definitions, most demons today
are free to roam about the universe unconfined, doing Satan's
bidding. Ephesians 6:12 unveils the demonic forces arrayed
against God's people: "For we are not fighting against flesh-
and-blood enemies, but against evil rulers and authorities of
the unseen world, against mighty powers in this dark world,
and against evil spirits in the heavenly places." Presently, the
majority of demonic spirits aren't in any part of the underworld, much less the final lake of fire. Satan is also free and
roams the earth "like a roaring lion, looking for someone
to devour" (1 Peter 5:8). Only some demons are presently
locked in the abyss or Tartarus. As Pastor Skip Heitzig says,
"This might shock you, but Satan is not in hell; in fact, he
has never been in hell, and he won't be there until the end
of Revelation. When God finally consigns the devil to hell,
Satan won't be its king; but rather, he will be tormented more
than anyone else."[14]

The idea of Satan and demons torturing humans in hell
is foreign to God's Word. Donald Grey Barnhouse notes,
"When Satan finally reaches Hell he will be there as the chief
victim of punishment and not in any sense as the ruler or the
one who causes the torture. The important thing about Hell
is that God runs it, and we must never forget that fact. There
is not a line in the Bible that shows that the devil has ever
been to Hell, and there is no line in the Bible that says that

when he gets there he or his minions will have any authority."[15] Satan and demons aren't in hell yet, and even when they are cast there at the end of Christ's millennial reign, they won't be in charge.

Baxter claims that she saw souls chained to one another being dragged "under the surface of the lake of fire."[16] The Bible says that no one is presently in the lake of fire. The lake of fire won't be populated until after the Battle of Armageddon, when its first two occupants will be cast there—the Antichrist and the false prophet (see Revelation 19:20). Additionally, Jesus is never associated with hell in the New Testament. Jesus resides in heaven. There's no evidence whatsoever that Jesus leads tours of the netherworld, as Baxter asserts.

Highway to Hell

During her time in hell, Baxter says she met a man who asked Jesus to let him go back to earth to tell his relatives to repent of their sins while they are still alive. She quotes the response of Jesus to the man:

> Jesus said, "They have preachers, teachers, elders—
> all ministering the gospel. They will tell them.
> They also have the advantages of the modern
> communications systems and many other ways to
> learn of Me. I sent workers to them that they might
> believe and be saved. If they will not believe when

they hear the gospel, neither will they be persuaded though one rises from the dead."[17]

Baxter is correctly quoting the words of Jesus from Luke 16, but then violates what he said by claiming that Jesus took her to hell so that *she* could come back and warn us not to end up there. While it is true that she doesn't claim to rise from the dead, Jesus' main point in the parable seems to be that we don't need people coming back from hell to warn us how bad it is. Luke 16:27-31 says,

> The rich man said, "Please, Father Abraham, at least send him to my father's home. For I have five brothers, and I want him to warn them so they don't end up in this place of torment."
> But Abraham said, "Moses and the prophets have warned them. Your brothers can read what they wrote."
> The rich man replied, "No, Father Abraham! But if someone is sent to them from the dead, then they will repent of their sins and turn to God."
> But Abraham said, "If they won't listen to Moses and the prophets, they won't listen even if someone rises from the dead."

Jesus is emphasizing in Luke 16 that his Word is sufficient to warn sinners about hell and to lead them to repentance. The claim by both Baxter and Wiese that Jesus told them he needed them to experience hell's torments in order to tell others about it contradicts the clear teaching of Jesus that his Word is enough. One of the first pages of *A Divine Revelation of Hell* records a purported message from Jesus to Mary K. Baxter: "To Kathryn from Jesus: For this purpose you were born, to write and tell what I have shown and told you. For these things are faithful and true. Your call is to let the world know there is a hell and that I, Jesus, was sent by God to save them from this torment."[18] Why would Jesus say this to her when he has already told us in Luke 16 that he won't send people back from hell to tell others about it?

Let me repeat what I said about the heaven-and-back books. The Bible is our source—our *only* reliable source—about hell, heaven, and life after death. God has told us what he wants us to know. As his children, we need to humbly accept his decision to reveal what he wants us to know about life after death. In his hellish memoir, Wiese says, "My horrifying journey felt like it lasted an eternity, but, in actuality, it lasted less than half an hour. Those twenty-three minutes were more than enough to convince me that I would never, ever want to return, not even for one more minute."[19] But isn't the Bible enough to get us to the same place? A reading of the Bible's description of hell should be plenty to convince any serious person that one would never want to go to hell for even a minute. Going beyond what is written is a not-so-subtle demonstration of our lack of trust in God to tell us what we need to know. We're saying to our infinite, sovereign Father that we need more. Let's stay far away from this trap, accepting what we have in God's Word, not rest-lessly searching for more answers in books that contradict what the Bible says.

CHAPTER 9

WHAT IS HEAVEN LIKE?

Only in heaven will we know exactly what heaven is like.
BILLY GRAHAM

THROUGHOUT THIS BOOK I have emphasized over and over again that we have to stick to the Scriptures when it comes to information about heaven and the afterlife. If that's true, then this question arises: What *does* the Bible say about heaven? How is it described? For every believer, this question is far from theoretical. Heaven is our eternal destination.

A few years ago, my wife, Cheryl, and I were invited to travel to Australia. We were leaving our home to travel a long way (a *very* long way)—to a new hemisphere. For a few months before we departed, I spent time learning about Sydney's history and key sites. I consulted every travel brochure I could get my hands on. It would have been strange if we'd had no interest in learning about the place we were visiting. In a much greater way, it would be unthinkable for a believer in Jesus Christ to have little curiosity or interest in learning about his or her heavenly home. As J. C. Ryle says, "I pity that man who never thinks about heaven. . . . Cold and unfeeling must that heart be which never gives a thought to that dwelling-place! Dull and earthly must that mind be which never considers heaven!"[1] We should eagerly seek all the biblical information about heaven we can get.

In this chapter I want to take a brief tour of our eternal home, not in a mystical dream or vision or near-death experience but in the pages of God's inspired Word—his heavenly travel brochure.

I like the way Randy Alcorn views the relationship between life on earth now and the life to come in heaven: "Eternal life will be enjoying forever what life on Earth is at its finest moments, what it was intended to be. Since in Heaven we'll finally experience life at its best, it would be more accurate to call our present existence the *beforelife* rather than what follows the *afterlife*."[2] Our life now is the *beforelife*; heaven will be life in its fullest sense.

For a believer in Jesus Christ, the worst thing that can happen to us is the best thing that can happen to us. The worst thing, from our perspective, is death, but the best thing is going to heaven to be with Christ. Heaven is our home. Everything we love is there or will be there.

When theologian John Owen was soon to die, his secretary began to write to his friend in Owen's name, "I am still in the land of the living." Owen stopped her and offered a correction. "Change that and say, I am yet in the land of the dying, but I hope soon to be in the land of the living."[3] We think we are in the land of the living going to the land of the dying. But really we're in the land of the dying, going to the land of the living.

For Heaven's Sake

When thinking about heaven, we need to remember that the Bible teaches there are three "heavens" (sorry, for all it's talked about, there is no seventh heaven). The first heaven is the atmospheric heaven where the birds and airplanes fly. The second heaven is the stellar heaven where the sun, moon, and stars are suspended in space. The third heaven is the abode of God. The apostle Paul says he was caught up to the third heaven, where God dwells (see 2 Corinthians 12:2, 4). The third heaven is home for God, angels, and the souls of redeemed humans. When a believer dies, his or her soul (the immaterial part) goes immediately to heaven (see 2 Corinthians 5:8; Philippians 1:23). Heaven is described in Scripture as a glorious city, the new Jerusalem (see Hebrews 11:10, 16; Revelation 21:2).

The Bible describes heaven for us, but we still struggle to really understand its majesty and grandeur. People have come up with all kinds of ways to describe it in a way we can grasp. I read this description a while back about the stark contrast between heaven and hell:

Hell: where the police are German, the cooks British, the mechanics French, the lovers Swiss, and it is all organized and run by the Italians.

Heaven: where the police are British, the cooks are French, the mechanics are German, the lovers are Italian, and it is all organized and run by the Swiss.

Heaven will be much better than that. J. C. Ryle summarizes heaven beautifully:

Heaven is the eternal presence of everything that can make a saint happy, and the eternal absence of everything that can cause sorrow. Sickness, and pain, and disease, and death, and poverty, and labour, and money, and care, and ignorance, and misunderstanding, and slander, and lying, and strife, and contention, and quarrels, and envies, and jealousies, and bad tempers, and infidelity, and scepticism, and irreligion, and superstition, and heresy, and schism, and wars, and fightings, and bloodshed, and murders, and law suits—all, all these things shall have no place in heaven. On earth, in this present time, they may live and flourish. In heaven their very footprints shall not be known.[4]

Years ago, I read this about heaven: "All that is bad will be absent and all that is good will be present. The curse will be removed. The blessing of God will be known in a manifest and multiplied way. Night will not cloud its day. Death will not walk its streets. Tears will not seep through its walls. Sickness will not enter its gates. Sin will not curse its history. The devil will not bother its citizens."

Paul Enns provides this enlightening summary of what it means to go to heaven:

In Heaven . . .

1. Our existence continues.
2. We shall never die.
3. We are in our new home.
4. Angels will escort us.
5. Christ will welcome us.
6. We will be with Christ.
7. We will be reunited with loved ones.
8. We will be home.
9. We will be where Jesus wants us to be.[5]

Heaven Today

To fully understand heaven, it's important to recognize that heaven today—often called the intermediate heaven—is different from the eternal state. When a believer dies today, the soul goes immediately to the Lord's presence in the new Jerusalem or heavenly city. God's eternal throne is in this celestial city, which is described in Revelation 21:10–22:5.

These verses describe the indescribable. Here are a few of the features of the heavenly city that are highlighted.

The Glory of God. The main feature of this city is that it has the glory of God (see Revelation 21:11, 23). It is described in terms of light, precious stones, and gold polished to mirror brilliance. The celestial skyline dazzles as the light of God shines on the beauty of the city. The glory of God will be overpowering and overwhelming. The city is a colossal cube—1,400 miles long, wide, and deep. It contains 2.74 billion cubic miles of space—enough to hold nearly 100,000 billion people. How big is that? To help us envision it, we can think of a map of the United States. The giant footprint of the city would be about the same as drawing a line from Miami up to Maine, then westward to Minneapolis, then south to Houston, and then back to Miami. And that's just the ground level! The towering city rises 1,400 miles as well.

The city is like one huge Holy of Holies. Remember that in the ancient Tabernacle the Holy of Holies, where God's glory dwelled, was a fifteen-foot cube. Later in the Temple, the dwelling place of God was a thirty-foot cube. The heavenly city is a 1,400-mile cube that's the holy dwelling place of God.

The Wall of Jasper. The wall is for protection, security, and separation. It is 216-feet thick and 1,400 miles high and is made of jasper, which probably refers to a diamond or a gem that looks like ice. The wall looks like a shimmering sheet of ice.

The Twelve Gates. The gates of the city, which are never

closed, provide open access and entrance for the Lord's people (see Revelation 21:25). Each gate is made from a single pearl. The names of the twelve tribes of Israel are inscribed on the gates. Stop and think for a moment about the lives of the twelve sons of Jacob that the tribes were named after. They were devious, sinful men who sold their brother Joseph into slavery and lied to their bereaved, aged father. Genesis 38, which recounts the sins of Judah, is one of the most sordid chapters in the Bible. The fact that God etches the names of these men on the gates of his holy, heavenly city is an eternal witness to God's amazing grace. The names on the gates of heaven should reassure us all that "even the worst sort of sinners can enter heaven by God's redemptive grace."[6]

The Twelve Foundation Stones. The foundation stones reveal the permanence of the city (see Hebrews 11:10). They are inlaid with twelve precious gems: jasper (diamond), sapphire (deep blue), agate (green), emerald (green), onyx (layered stone of red), carnelian (blood red), chrysolite (golden yellow), beryl (sea green), topaz (greenish gold or yellow), chrysoprase (gold green), jacinth (violet), and amethyst (purple quartz).

The Street. People often talk about the streets of gold in heaven, but actually there is only one street of gold. Everyone will live on Main Street, and that street will be paved with gold polished to mirror brilliance. Gold is so plentiful to the Creator that he uses it to pave his street.

A River. A river of crystal-clear water will run down Main Street from the throne of God.

The Tree of Life. The tree that man was excluded from when he was expelled from the Garden of Eden will be available to all of God's people for all of eternity.

Thinking of the heavenly city, one of today's Christian composers says it well: "I can only imagine."[7]

Heaven's Main Attraction

There will be nothing but the best in the heavenly city. There will not be any cinder blocks, shag carpet, or cheap imitations. Only the best will be used. The heavenly city is the place in John 14:1-3 that Jesus was going to prepare for us. It is the Father's house in which there are many dwelling places. Jesus has been working on it now for two thousand years. What a place it will be! Above all, it is the dwelling place of God. As D. L. Moody once said, "It is not the jeweled walls or pearly gates that are going to make heaven attractive. It is being with God." As someone once said, "We know very little about heaven, but we could best describe it as an unknown region with a well-known inhabitant." There is not a better way to think of heaven than that. God himself is what will make heaven heaven. John MacArthur explains,

> Heaven is *his* realm. He has gone there to prepare
> a place for us. That truth is what makes heaven so
> precious for the Christian. Our eternity there will be
> an eternity in the presence of Christ, sharing warm
> fellowship with him personally, and living forever in

the light of his countenance. That is heaven's chief
appeal for any Christian whose priorities are straight.
Christ himself *is* the glory of heaven.[8]

For this reason every believer should feel the heavenward
pull, the tug of heaven. Our feet are on earth but our hearts
are to be in heaven, where Christ dwells (see Colossians
3:1-4). Thinking about heaven should rest at the center of
our worldview and should motivate us to live for the Lamb
of glory who dwells in unapproachable light yet who made a
way for us to dwell with him forever by shedding his blood
on the cross and rising from the dead.

The New Heaven and New Earth

The heavenly city, the new Jerusalem, is the present abode of
God, angels, and the souls of deceased believers. But someday,
after the second coming of Jesus and his one-thousand-year
reign on the earth, God will destroy this present universe and
create a brand-new one. After the present order is destroyed,
God will put it all back together again. What all the king's
horses and all the king's men could not do for Humpty
Dumpty, God will do for the universe. He will gather all the
building blocks of the original creation and make a brand-
new universe. Revelation 21:1-5 describes the scene:

> I saw a new heaven and a new earth, for the old
> heaven and the old earth had disappeared. And the

sea was also gone. And I saw the holy city, the new Jerusalem, coming down from God out of heaven like a bride beautifully dressed for her husband. I heard a loud shout from the throne, saying, "Look, God's home is now among his people! He will live with them, and they will be his people. God himself will be with them. He will wipe every tear from their eyes, and there will be no more death or sorrow or crying or pain. All these things are gone forever." And the one sitting on the throne said, "Look, I am making everything new!" And then he said to me, "Write this down, for what I tell you is trustworthy and true."

God will destroy the present created order and make way for the new creation. The creation of the new heaven and new earth is only mentioned in four places in the Bible: Isaiah 65:17; 66:22; 2 Peter 3:13; and Revelation 21:1. The word "new" in Revelation 21:1 is *kainos*, which denotes something not just new in time but new qualitatively. Something that is different and superior to the old. The new world will be created by a perfect God who does perfect work. It will be a perfect place existing in a perfect environment.

As John looks at the new heaven and new earth in his vision, the spotlight shifts suddenly to a descending metropolis, the new Jerusalem, the holy city, coming down from God. John sees this cubed city the size of a continent floating through space, approaching the new earth. I believe the heavenly city will come down and rest on the new earth and serve as the capital city of the new heaven and new earth. The new Jerusalem will be the capital of the eternal state. It will be the metropolis of eternity. The fact that this city is mentioned in conjunction with the new earth and that the city has huge foundation stones seems to suggest that it will rest on the new earth (see Hebrews 11:10).

The perfection of the new creation is magnified when contrasted to the original creation account in Genesis. What started in Genesis is brought to completion in Revelation. Everything will come full circle in eternity.

Genesis	Revelation
Heavens and earth created	New heaven and earth
Sun created	No sun
Night established	No night
Seas created	No seas
Rivers in the Garden of Eden	River in the new Jerusalem
Curse announced	No curse
Death enters	Death exits
Man denied access to the tree of life	Access to the tree of life restored
Sorrow and pain begin	Sorrow and pain end

What Will and Won't Be in Heaven

The Bible does not tell us a great deal about the new heaven and new earth, but what it does record is exciting. It is a place of perfection characterized both by what *is* there and what *is not* there.

THREE THINGS THAT WILL BE THERE

1. The holy city, new Jerusalem
2. God himself dwelling among his people
3. Righteousness (see 2 Peter 3:13)

THINGS THAT WILL NOT BE THERE

Charles Swindoll has searched the Scriptures and compiled a good list of twelve things that will not be in heaven:

1. No more sea—because all chaos and disorder (symbolized by the sea in ancient times) will be gone (21:1)
2. No more tears—because all hurt will be removed (21:4)
3. No more death—because mortality is swallowed up by life (21:4)
4. No more mourning—because all sorrow will be perfectly comforted (21:4)
5. No more crying—because joy will reign supreme (21:4)
6. No more pain—because all diseases will be expelled (21:4)
7. No more thirst—because every desire will be satisfied (21:6)
8. No more wickedness—because all evil will be banished (21:8, 27)

9. No more temple—because God will be everywhere (21:22)
10. No more night—because the glory of God will shine (21:23-25; 22:5)
11. No more closed gates—because God's door will always be open (21:25)
12. No more curse—because the death of Christ has lifted it (22:3)[9]

Based on this comforting list, some have described heaven as the blessed place of "no more." Steven Lawson has compiled an expanded list of "no mores":

There will be no funeral homes, no hospitals, no abortion clinics, no divorce courts, no brothels, no bankruptcy courts, no psychiatric wards, and no treatment centers.

There will be no pornography, no dial-a-porn, no teen suicide, no AIDS, no cancer, no talk shows, no rape, no missing children . . . no drug problems, no drive-by shootings, no racial tension, and no prejudice.

There will be no misunderstandings, no injustice, no depression, no hurtful words, no gossip, no hurt feelings, no worry, no emptiness, and no child abuse.

There will be no wars, no financial worries, no emotional heartaches, no physical pain, no spiritual flatness, no relational divisions, no murders, and no casseroles.

There will be no tears, no suffering, no separations, no starvation, no arguments, no accidents, no emergency departments, no doctors, no nurses, no heart monitors, no rust, no perplexing questions, no false teachers, no financial shortages, no hurricanes, no bad habits, no decay, and no locks.

We will never need to confess sin. Never need to apologize again. Never need to straighten out a strained relationship. Never have to resist Satan again. Never have to resist temptation. Never![10]

Who Will Be in Heaven?

There's a great line from an old spiritual that says, "Everybody talkin' 'bout heaven ain't goin' there." Mere talk about heaven won't get us there. The only thing that will get us to heaven is personal faith in Jesus Christ. Hebrews 12:22-24 gives a description of the inhabitants of God's new world:

> You have come to Mount Zion and to the city of the living God, the heavenly Jerusalem, and to myriads of angels, to the general assembly and church of the firstborn who are enrolled in heaven, and to God, the Judge of all, and to the spirits of *the* righteous made perfect, and to Jesus, the mediator of a new

covenant, and to the sprinkled blood, which speaks better than *the blood* of Abel. (NASB)

There are three identifiable groups in the new Jerusalem besides God himself and Jesus: angels, church-age believers ("the general assembly and church of the firstborn"), and the rest of the people of God from the other ages ("the spirits of the righteous made perfect"). All who by God's grace have trusted in the person and promises of God will be in heaven.

The Bible is clear about who will be in heaven, but it also leaves no doubt about who *won't* be there. Revelation 21:8 describes eight kinds of people who will not be there. The list does not refer to isolated acts of sin in these areas but describes the direction and pattern of one's life.

1. The cowards—those who are ashamed of Christ (Matthew 10:33).
2. Unbelievers—those who neglect or reject Christ.
3. The corrupt—those who live impure, polluted lives.
4. Murderers—those who practice murder. (A person who commits murder can be saved by God's grace. King David is a perfect example. This refers to people who practice murder and never seek God's forgiveness.)
5. The immoral—those who live a lifestyle of sexual sin outside the bonds of monogamous, heterosexual marriage.

6. Those who practice witchcraft—those who delve into occultic practices.
7. Idol worshipers—those who trust something within creation to give what only God can give. (An idol is not just a graven image but anything that absorbs the heart and imagination more than God. Colossians 3:5 says, "A greedy person is an idolater, worshiping the things of this world.")
8. Liars—those who habitually deceive and mislead others.

While these will be excluded, all of God's people of all the ages will have eternal access to the new heaven, the new earth, and the new Jerusalem. Of course, the key issue is—will *you* be there? Will you be a citizen of the new heaven and new earth and new Jerusalem? Heaven is a prepared place for a prepared people. Have you received God's offer of salvation? That is the key issue in all of life. It's fascinating to know what will happen to this world in the future, but it's much more important for you to know *your* future.

CHAPTER 10

HOW TO BE DEAD RIGHT

When I die I shall then have my greatest grief and my greatest joy—
my greatest grief that I have done so little for Jesus, and my greatest
joy that Jesus has done so much for me.
WILLIAM GRIMSHAW

SARAH WINCHESTER'S HUSBAND earned a fortune by manufacturing and selling the famous Winchester repeating rifles. When her husband died in 1918, Sarah relocated to San Jose, California. Sarah had long been curious about spiritism, and her mourning for her husband drove her to consult a medium to speak with him. The medium told her, "As long as you keep building your home, you will never die."

Sarah believed the medium so wholeheartedly that she bought an unfinished seventeen-room mansion and embarked on an incredible expansion project that continued until she died at the age of eighty-five. Her building efforts cost millions of dollars at a time when laborers earned fifty cents a day. Sarah's instructions were beyond eccentric. Each window was to have thirteen panes, each wall thirteen panels, each closet thirteen hooks, and each chandelier thirteen globes. The floor plan was chaotic, to say the least. Corridors snaked randomly, some leading nowhere. One door opened to a blank wall, another to a fifty-foot drop. One set of stairs led to a ceiling that had no door. There were trap doors, secret passageways, and eerie tunnels.

The "completed" estate sprawled over six acres and had six kitchens, thirteen bathrooms, forty stairways, forty-seven fireplaces, fifty-two skylights, four hundred sixty-seven doors, ten thousand windows, one hundred fifty rooms, and a bell tower. And Sarah had stockpiled enough building materials that they could have kept up construction for another eighty years![1]

Yet in spite of her tireless efforts, death came for Sarah Winchester. Death was never confused. It knew just where to find her. And it knows how and where to find each one of us when our time comes.

The Bottom Is Good

The searching question we all face is, what should *I* do? Will I be dead right or dead wrong? Where will I go? As we've seen, heaven and hell are both *for real*. Which will be real for you at the end of life? Doug Groothuis says it well: "In a precarious world, we are all 'near death.' According to Jesus, this means we are all either near hell or near heaven."[2] That means we need to always be ready. Jim Elliot, the martyred missionary, once said, "When it comes time to die, make sure that's all you have to do." In other words, live ready to die. Are you ready? Have you given up on saving yourself and come to Christ as your only hope of heaven and eternal life?

I love the scene in *The Pilgrim's Progress* where Christian and Hopeful come to the final river of death. They are gripped with fear that the water will be over their heads. But Hopeful goes first and calls back to Christian, "Be of good cheer, my brother; I feel the bottom, and it is good."

For every Christian, the bottom is good because of the word of Christ Jesus our Savior, who has promised that he gives the gift of forgiveness and eternal life to all who will receive him as their Savior and Lord. The gospel, which means "good news," is that while we are sinners, Jesus is our Savior. He came to earth and died in our place on the cross as our substitute. Carefully and prayerfully read these verses of Scripture, asking the Lord to make them real and living in your heart, and respond to their message if you've never done so before:

- "To all who believed him and accepted him, he gave the right to become children of God." (John 1:12)
- "Anyone who believes in God's Son has eternal life." (John 3:36)
- "Jesus told him, 'I am the way, the truth, and the life. No one can come to the Father except through me.'" (John 14:6)
- "When we were utterly helpless, Christ came at

just the right time and died for us sinners. . . . God showed his great love for us by sending Christ to die for us while we were still sinners." (Romans 5:6, 8)

• "God saved you by his grace when you believed. And you can't take credit for this; it is a gift from God. Salvation is not a reward for the good things we have done, so none of us can boast about it." (Ephesians 2:8-9)

Jesus promised he will take all believers to be with him in heaven (see John 14:3). When you face death, if Jesus doesn't come in your lifetime, trust in his promise to bring you safely to the other side.

One Shot

In 1892, the Buffalo Bill's Wild West toured Europe. Thousands of Europeans went to see the Wild West. One of the main attractions was Annie Oakley, who was known as "Little Sure Shot."

Annie Oakley had many amazing sharpshooting tricks as part of her act. These included shooting through and splitting several playing cards tossed up in the air before they landed. Another was to shoot a metal coin tossed into the air about twenty-seven yards away. Another Oakley staple was shooting an apple placed behind her using a mirror. Any male sharpshooter who challenged was soundly defeated. She was truly the first female superstar in show business.

One particular demonstration Annie had in her routine was to shoot the ashes off the tip of someone's cigar. The act would start with Oakley asking for volunteers from the audience. Typically no one would volunteer and her husband, Frank Butler, would finally consent to the stunt. At one Wild West performance, someone did stand up to volunteer. It was none other than the newly crowned German emperor Kaiser Wilhelm II. Before any of his entourage could talk the German emperor out of it, Kaiser Wilhelm II stood up, took out a cigar, lit it, and put it in his mouth. Annie Oakley knew quite well what she'd gotten herself into. With the cigar in the kaiser's mouth, ash at the end of it, Oakley took aim with her Colt 45. She pulled the trigger, the shot was fired, and the ash was blown off the cigar just a few inches in front of the kaiser's face.

Fifteen years later Kaiser Wilhelm plunged the world into its first world war, causing Annie Oakley to wonder how events might have unfolded had she unfortunately missed and hit the kaiser. What is known is that Annie Oakley did send the kaiser a letter after the start of World War I, asking for the opportunity to take another shot.

She never received a reply.

I've thought about that story quite a bit, and it teaches us a very important lesson: you only get one shot.

You only get one shot at life. There are no do-overs. There's no dress rehearsal. Make sure to take dead aim with your life. Make sure you have received Jesus Christ and are living faithfully for him.

Make your one shot count for eternity.

Appendix 1: Answers to Common Questions about Death and Heaven

Death for the Christian cuts the cord that holds us captive in this present
evil world so that angels may transport believers to their heavenly
inheritance. Death is the fiery chariot, the gentle voice of the King,
the invitation to nonstop passage into the banquet house of the world
of glory.

BILLY GRAHAM

1. What Happens When You Die?

More Americans than ever (about 80 percent) now say that they believe in life after death. Since the turn of the century, belief in an afterlife among US Catholics, Jews, and those with no religious affiliation has grown significantly. However, as more people profess to believe in life after death, it doesn't seem that most people have much of an idea about what happens to people when they die. Every year my family and I vacation in Ruidoso, New Mexico. At one place we frequent, there's an imitation "boot hill" that's littered with humorous tombstones. One of my favorites goes like this:

Here lies Lester Moore
Four slugs from a .44
No Les. No more.

This is good humor but bad theology. Somewhere, more or less, Les Moore lives. Or to put it another way, Les is more. We all end up somewhere.

Death in the Bible always means separation, not annihilation or cessation of existence. In the Garden of Eden, God told Adam that if he or his wife ate of the fruit of the tree of the knowledge of good and evil, they would surely die. When they partook of the forbidden fruit, God's warning was fulfilled, and they immediately died spiritually—that is, they were separated from God. Adam and Eve tried to hide themselves from God because they were aware of their sin. Many years later, as a result of sin, they died physically. Spiritual death in the Bible is spiritual separation of the soul and spirit from God.

Likewise, when a person dies physically, he or she does not cease to exist, but experiences a separation. Physical death brings about a separation between the material part (body) and immaterial part (soul/spirit) of the person. When this separation occurs, the body "falls asleep" and is buried, but the immaterial part of the person immediately goes to one of two places—Hades or heaven—depending on the person's relationship with Christ. The departed spirit of a believer in Christ goes immediately into the presence of the Lord. Several passages of Scripture make this clear:

- Luke 16:19-22: "There was a certain rich man who was splendidly clothed in purple and fine linen and who lived each day in luxury. At his gate lay a poor man named Lazarus who was covered with sores. As Lazarus lay there longing for scraps from the rich man's table, the dogs would come and lick his open sores. Finally, the poor man died and was carried by the angels to be with Abraham."

- 2 Corinthians 5:8, NASB: "We are of good courage, I say, and prefer rather to be absent from the body and to be at home with the Lord."
- Philippians 1:21, 23, NASB: "To me, to live is Christ and to die is gain. . . . But I am hard-pressed from both *directions*, having the desire to depart and be with Christ, for *that* is very much better."

When Christ comes at the Rapture for his people, the perfected spirits of the redeemed will return with the Lord from heaven be reunited with their resurrected, glorified bodies (see 1 Thessalonians 4:14-16).

When an unbeliever dies, his or her departed spirit goes immediately into Hades to experience conscious, unrelenting torment. Jesus told the Parable of the Rich Man and Lazarus (recorded in Luke 16:19-31). When the unbelieving rich man dies, his soul is transported instantly to Hades. "The rich man also died and was buried, and his soul went to the place of the dead. There, in torment, he saw Abraham in the far distance with Lazarus at his side. (Luke 16:22-23). At the Great White Throne Judgment (see Revelation 20:11-15), the bodies of all the lost will be resurrected and joined with their spirits to appear before the Judge of the universe. At that point they will be cast into the lake of fire, where they will experience what the Bible calls the "second death" (Revelation 20:6, 14). The second death, or what we might call eternal death, is eternal separation of the lost from the loving presence of God. They will be banished from him forever (see 2 Thessalonians 1:8-9).

When thinking about the death of a believer in Jesus Christ, I love the poem "Gone from My Sight," written by Henry Van Dyke:

> *I am standing upon the seashore. A ship, at my side,*
> *spreads her white sails to the moving breeze and starts*
> *for the blue ocean. She is an object of beauty and strength.*
> *I stand and watch her until, at length, she hangs like a*
> *   speck*
> *of white cloud just where the sun and sky come to mingle*
> *   with each other.*
>
> *Then someone at my side says, "There, she is gone!"*
>
> *Gone where?*
>
> *Gone from my sight. That is all. She is just as large in*
> *   mast,*
> *hull and spar as she was when she left my side.*
> *And, she is just as able to bear her load of living freight to*
> *   her destined port.*
> *Her diminished size is in me—not in her.*

And, just at the moment when someone says, "There, she is gone,"
there are other eyes watching her coming, and other voices ready to take up the glad shout, "Here she comes!"

2. Will We Know Each Other in Heaven?

Almost every person who believes in heaven has probably thought about the answer to this question at one time or another. We all have people we love dearly who have died as believers in Christ, and we wonder if we will recognize our friends and loved ones in heaven and if they will know us. Scripture teaches that we *will* know one another in the afterlife. In the Parable of the Rich Man and Lazarus, Jesus says the rich man, who is in Hades, recognizes Lazarus in heaven and remembers all the facts about their relationship on earth. The rich man even remembers his five brothers who are still on earth.

In the Old Testament account of Abraham's death, we read these comforting words: "He died at a ripe old age, having lived a long and satisfying life. He breathed his last and joined his ancestors in death" (Genesis 25:8). Some translations read, "And he was gathered to his people." This same phrase is repeated for Ishmael (see Genesis 25:17), Isaac (see Genesis 35:29), and Jacob (see Genesis 49:33). Joining their ancestors in death or being gathered to their people implies that we will know our ancestors and family when we arrive in heaven, and they will know us.

Scripture also seems to teach that we will even recognize people we never met here on earth. When Jesus was transfigured before Peter, James, and John on Mount Hermon, Moses and Elijah appeared with Jesus (see Matthew 17:1-4). According to Scripture, Peter immediately recognized the two men with Jesus as Moses and Elijah. Obviously, Peter had never met Moses and Elijah. They were gone centuries before he was born. So how did he know who they were? Apparently he possessed an intuitive knowledge that enabled him to immediately know their identities. Since the Transfiguration is a picture of the Lord's second coming (see 2 Peter 1:16-18), it may be telling us that it will be the same way in heaven. All of us will possess the intuitive ability to recognize others in heaven—even people we never knew on earth.

In one sense we could correctly say that we won't really know each other *until* we get to heaven. Only in heaven, with all the posing and pretense removed, will we really know one another and enjoy the intimate, unhindered fellowship God intended for us all along. I like the story of a woman in England who was a believer and who suffered a great tragedy when her adult daughter died. She traveled by ship to visit her other daughter in New York, and during the voyage, the ship encountered some terrible storms. For a while it looked like they could go down. Throughout the ordeal, she was calm, serene, and filled with peace. A young man asked her how she could be so calm, and she replied, "I have a daughter in New York and a daughter in heaven, and it doesn't matter to me which one I go see." We need to have faith that when we leave this earth, we are not just leaving loved ones behind but are going to meet those who have gone before us.

3. Will We Know Everything in Heaven?

In many of the heaven-and-back books the authors claim they were given special insight and knowledge in heaven. I'm sure every one of us realizes how limited our present knowledge is and long to know more. It seems as we go through life and learn more, we become increasingly aware of how much we don't know. Increased knowledge and understanding of the mysteries of life is one thing we probably all hope is part of heaven.

Most people probably assume we will know much more in heaven than we know here—that just makes sense. But how much will we know? Will we immediately know everything? Will there be a mass knowledge transfer or "information dump" into our consciousness that reveals all the mysteries of God?

The Bible teaches that God is infinite. Every attribute or characteristic that God possesses, he possesses to an infinite degree. God's infinite knowledge is often referred to as omniscience—that is, God knows everything. When we get to heaven, if we know everything, that would make *us* omniscient, which is true only of God. Only the infinite can know everything. God will always be infinite, and we will always be finite. Angels in heaven, who are perfect creatures, don't know everything. They are constantly learning more and more about God and his ways (see 1 Peter 1:12). So I don't believe we will know everything in heaven.

Having said that, when we get to heaven, both our minds and bodies will be glorified, perfected, and exponentially enhanced. Part of that enhancement will be a capacity to know and understand that is far beyond anything we experience on earth (see 1 Corinthians 13:12). Part of our unending experience in heaven will be learning more about God and his ways. For all eternity we will always be learning more about the wonders and majesty of our great God and his creation.

Peter Kreeft makes this observation: "When you come to think of it, knowing everything would be more like Hell than Heaven for us. For one thing, we need progress and hope: we need to look forward to knowing something new tomorrow. Mystery is our mind's food. . . . Only omnipotence can bear the burden of omniscience; only God's shoulders are strong enough to carry the burden of infinite knowledge without losing the joy."[1] We will never know everything, but we will know and learn things we never imagined here on earth. (I may even become good at math.) We will learn the answers to the nagging questions of this life and answers to questions we never even thought to ask. God will open up new vistas we never even imagined.

4. How Can We Enjoy Heaven Knowing People Are in Hell?

This is a very difficult question for me. The Bible is clear that heaven is a place of eternal happiness, peace, rest, joy, and delight where there are no tears, crying, or sorrow (see

Revelation 21:4). Yet the Bible also says hell is a tragic reality for all who reject Jesus Christ. So how can believers in heaven experience unmitigated joy knowing people are in hell?

Some answer this sobering question by proposing that God will permanently erase the earthly memories of his people in heaven so that any remembrance of loved ones and friends who are in hell will be unknown. Others say that people in heaven won't even know that hell exists. Support for this view is based on several biblical passages: Deuteronomy 25:19; Psalms 9:5; 69:28; 109:13. Primary support for this view is drawn from Isaiah 65:17-19:

> Look! I am creating new heavens and a new earth,
>   and no one will even think about the old ones
>   anymore.
> Be glad; rejoice forever in my creation!
>   And look! I will create Jerusalem as a place
>   of happiness.
>   Her people will be a source of joy.
> I will rejoice over Jerusalem
>   and delight in my people.
> And the sound of weeping and crying
>   will be heard in it no more.

The main point in this passage seems to be that in our glorified state, everything will be so awe-inspiring that the sorrows and tears of this life will be completely overshadowed, not that we won't remember our lives on earth. Maintaining that our memories in heaven will be wiped clean would mean that in some ways we would know more on earth than we do in heaven, which doesn't seem likely. This answer is unsatisfactory to me.

My best answer to this question is threefold. First, we have to believe that we will be happy in heaven despite the existence of hell. God has promised that we will be happy in heaven, and we can rest assured that God has the power to fulfill what he's promised. Charles Spurgeon once said that our new resurrection body won't have tear glands because they won't be necessary. I like that.

Second, when we get to heaven, we'll possess a perfected spirit with an ability to see things clearly from the divine perspective. As Ron Rhodes observes, "We will be aware of the full justice of God's decisions. We will clearly see that those who are in hell are there precisely because they rejected God's only provision for escaping hell. They are those to whom God ultimately says, 'Thy will be done.'"[2]

In heaven, for the first time in our existence, we'll see sin in the unapproachable light of God's holiness and will understand the extent of what it means for unbelievers to be Christ-rejecting enemies of God who spurned his gracious offer of salvation. We will also understand that we do not deserve to be in his presence either. God's undiminished justice and holiness and his undeserved grace and mercy will flood our being.

Third, there will be degrees of punishment in hell just as there are degrees of reward in heaven. God will mete out judgment and punishment in keeping with his perfect wisdom. God is infinitely wise and just. He knows what he's doing. We can calmly rest in his wisdom and justice, even concerning things we don't fully understand in this life.

5. Can People in Heaven See What's Happening on Earth?

At one time or another we've all probably wondered if our deceased friends or relatives are looking down on us. During an interview after an athletic event, one of the players or coaches who just lost a loved one will often say something like, "I know that my father was looking down today as we played that game." Statements like that sound good and often make us feel better, but are they true?

The Bible never answers this question specifically, but it does hint that people in heaven can see at least some of the events transpiring on earth. Hebrews 12:1 is often used to support the idea that departed believers in heaven are watching events on earth. The preceding chapter (Hebrews 11) is often called the biblical "Hall of Faith." In this famous chapter, the inspiring, courageous acts of faith by men like Enoch, Abraham, and Moses and women like Sarah and Rahab are highlighted. Following the faith chapter, the writer to the Hebrews concludes, "Since we are surrounded by such a huge crowd of witnesses to the life of faith, let us strip off every weight that slows us down, especially the sin that so easily trips us up. And let us run with endurance the race God has set before us" (Hebrews 12:1).

The "huge crowd of witnesses" is often envisioned as fans

in the stands cheering at a college football game looking down at those of us on the playing field of life as we run the particular race in life that God has given us to run. While this explanation sounds appealing, I believe it has the meaning reversed. The emphasis in Hebrews 12:1-2 is on those who have gone before us as a cloud of witnesses that *we* watch and seek to emulate. As we look back on the patient endurance and faithfulness in their lives recorded in Hebrews 11, they serve as witnesses to motivate us to emulate their lives. They are witnesses to us of God's approval of the life of faith.

Four main biblical passages indicate that believers in heaven can see and know at least some things happening on earth. First, when the deceased prophet Samuel comes back from the dead and appears to King Saul, he is aware of some of the events occurring in the life of Saul and in Saul's kingdom (see 1 Samuel 28:16-18). Second, Luke 15:7, 10 teaches that there's rejoicing in heaven over the salvation of a sinner on earth. The rejoicing seems to include angels in heaven as well as believers, which indicates they're aware of the salvation of sinners. Third, the martyrs in heaven in Revelation 6:9-10 are aware that their persecutors are still alive on earth. Fourth, Revelation 19:1-6 records the "hallelujah chorus" in heaven as a great multitude praises God for the destruction of Babylon on earth. The celebration indicates the inhabitants of heaven are well aware of Babylon's demise.

These four examples are enough to inform us we will know at least some of what's happening on earth but not enough for us to say we will know everything that happens.

I'm sure we will follow events we do know about on earth with intense interest.

Some might wonder why God would allow believers in heaven to see what's happening on earth. After all, with all the sin, sorrow, and misery in this world, this could easily eclipse our happiness and enjoyment in heaven. Seeing events on earth won't all be positive, but with our renewed, heavenly perspective, we must be able to handle seeing some things on earth or God wouldn't allow it.

Here's one final thought on this issue. When we're in heaven, we probably won't be as interested in what's happening on earth as we might think. We will be so enthralled and enraptured with heaven and our Lord that we'll be consumed with our new home and the Lamb of glory.

6. How Old Will We Appear to Be in Heaven?

The subject of age or appearance of age in heaven is never directly addressed in the Bible, so the answer to this question requires us to speculate based on other information. Two biblical passages help guide our thinking about this issue. First, Adam and Eve, like the rest of creation, were created in a fully mature state by God. We can safely assume that Adam and Eve were created at the ideal stage of physical development because God declared that they, along with the rest of his creation, were "very good" (see Genesis 1:31). Whatever physical stage Adam and Eve were in that corresponds to our years on earth will be the "age" we appear to be in heaven.

Second, assuming the death and resurrection of Jesus occurred in AD 33, Jesus was at least thirty-five years old when he died and possibly as old as thirty-seven or thirty-eight. After his resurrection Jesus repeatedly appeared to his followers in a body they recognized, so he must have looked similar to how he looked before he died and appeared to be about the same age. Scripture teaches that when we receive our new, glorified, resurrection bodies, they will be like Jesus' resurrection body (see Philippians 3:20-21). We can't necessarily conclude this means our new bodies will look like we did in our thirties, but we can know that our new bodies will be perfect in every way, just like the resurrection body of Jesus.

From these examples, I believe we can safely say that our Lord will give us a body that reflects how we looked in the prime and peak of our earthly life. For those who leave this earth before reaching the optimal age and condition, we can trust that our Lord, who knows everything, will fit them with a perfect body that reflects how they would have appeared at the optimal stage of human life on earth.

7. Are There Animals in Heaven?

In recent years many books have been written addressing this question. Almost everyone who has a pet they love wonders if they will see their companion in heaven. I've been asked this question many times. From my experience, this question is one of the most asked about life in heaven. As you can imagine, this question arouses strong emotions in those who deeply love their pets. In a well-known magazine focused on end-times prophecy, a question was submitted about the presence of animals in heaven. In answering the question, the magazine editor said, "Incidentally, the issue of animals in heaven has generated more responses than any other subject."[3]

I find it interesting but not surprising that so many people ask this question. I think that all Christians would agree that seeing our pets in heaven should not be our focus. Seeing our Lord and our loved ones and friends is our greatest desire. The Lamb of God will undoubtedly be our focus. However, this does not mean we won't enjoy the beauty of heavenly paradise, and part of the beauty and enjoyment could include our pets from here on earth.

Many people belittle the idea of animals in heaven and don't think anyone should even consider the issue. The main biblical argument against animals in heaven is Genesis 2:7, which says, "The LORD God formed the man from the dust of the ground. He breathed the breath of life into the man's nostrils, and the man became a living person [soul]." The Bible never says that God breathed life into animals and they became living souls, so the argument is that animals don't have souls. I disagree with this conclusion. The Bible affirms from beginning to end that animals have souls. Genesis 1:20, 24 uses the Hebrew word for "soul" (*nepes*) for animals. This word refers to the passionate appetites and desires of all living things including the drives for sex and food.[4] Additionally, in Revelation 8:9, the Greek word for "soul" (*psuchas*) is used in reference to sea creatures. However, to be fair, this word can sometimes carry the more general meaning of physical life. Obviously, almost every Christian would agree that the soul of an animal is qualitatively very different from the soul of a human being. The human soul craves God as well as sex and food. Nevertheless, the notion that animals have souls could allow for the fact that all or at least some of them will be resurrected to populate the new heaven and new earth.

I wholeheartedly agree that Scripture never says specifically whether our pets will be in heaven, but there are two main points that may indicate animals in general and pets in particular will be in heaven.

First, we have to remember that animals were part of the original creation of God that was declared "good" (see Genesis 1:25). The Garden of Eden was filled with animals. Revelation tells us that heaven will contain many of the same things that were in the original creation such as a river, trees, and fruit. Since that's true, why wouldn't animals also be part of the new creation? Animals are a vital ingredient of earthly life and strongly evidence the creative, imaginative genius of God who created the giraffe, rhinoceros, camel, lion, hummingbird, swan, whale, and octopus. W. A. Criswell says, "God has shown a penchant for varieties of life forms, and it would be difficult to imagine that this would not be perpetuated in the heavenlies."[5]

Addressing the fundamental question of animals in heaven, Peter Kreeft says, "The simplest answer is: Why not? How irrational is the prejudice that would allow plants (green fields and flowers) but not animals into Heaven!"[6] Dealing with the more difficult issue of whether the same animals will be in heaven that are here on earth, Kreeft adds,

> Would the same animals be in Heaven as on earth? "Is my dead cat in heaven?" Again, why not? God can raise up the very grass; why not cats? Though the blessed have better things to do than play with pets, the better does not exclude the lesser. We were meant from the beginning to have stewardship over the animals; we have not fulfilled that divine plan yet on earth; therefore it seems likely that the right relationship with animals will be part of Heaven; proper "petship." And what better place to begin than with already petted pets?[7]

Interestingly, C. S. Lewis maintained that animals belonging to believers are saved in and through their masters as a part of their extended family.[8]

A second argument for the presence of animals in heaven is that in the millennial kingdom, or thousand-year reign of Christ on earth, animals will populate the earth in abundance. Animal life in the Kingdom is depicted in Isaiah 11:6-8:

> In that day the wolf and the lamb will live together;
> the leopard will lie down with the baby goat.
> The calf and the yearling will be safe with the lion,
> and a little child will lead them all.

The cow will graze near the bear.
    The cub and the calf will lie down together.
    The lion will eat hay like a cow.
The baby will play safely near the hole of a cobra.
    Yes, a little child will put its hand in a nest of deadly
        snakes without harm.

The thousand-year reign of Christ on earth is not heaven or the eternal state, but it is phase one, or what we might call the "front porch," of the eternal Kingdom of God. Since animals will be present on earth in the Millennium, it follows that animals may populate the eternal state or new earth that God will create (see Revelation 21:1).

Joni Eareckson Tada, in her book *Holiness in Hidden Places*, talks about whether she will see her pet schnauzer, Scrappy, in heaven. Her words are a poignant summary of this issue:

> If God brings our pets back to life, it wouldn't
> surprise me. It would be just like Him. It would be
> totally in keeping with His generous character. . . .
> Exorbitant. Excessive. Extravagant in grace after
> grace. Of all the dazzling discoveries and ecstatic
> pleasures heaven will hold for us, the potential of
> seeing Scrappy would be pure whimsy—utterly,
> joyfully, surprisingly superfluous. . . . Heaven is
> going to be a place that will refract and reflect in as
> many ways as possible the goodness and joy of our

great God, who delights in lavishing love on His children.[9]

The best answer I've heard for this question came years ago at a prophecy conference I attended. Dr. John Walvoord was part of a panel answering questions from the audience. During the Q&A, a woman came to the microphone and said that her beloved Labrador had died recently, and she wanted to know if she would see him again in heaven. All the members of the panel on stage passed the microphone around and gave fairly detailed biblical, theological answers to the question. Dr. Walvoord was the final person to answer her question, and he asked her if it would make heaven happier for her if her dog was there. She nodded her head and said, "Oh, yes, it would make me so happy!" Then Dr. Walvoord replied, "If it will make you happier for him to be there, then he will be there."

What a great answer. All that will increase our happiness will be in heaven. All that decreases it will be absent.

8. What Will We Do in Heaven?

This frequently asked question often takes various forms, such as "Will there be football in heaven?" or "Will I be able to golf in heaven?" or "Will I get bored in heaven?" or "Will I sit around all day on a cloud strumming a harp?"

While the Bible doesn't tell us as much as we would like to know about what we will do in heaven, it does focus on six main things we will do.[10]

1. We will worship without distraction (Revelation 4:8-11; 7:10; 11:16-18; 15:2-4; 19:1-8).

2. We will serve without exhaustion (Revelation 7:14-15; 22:3).

3. We will rule without failure (Luke 19:17, 19; 1 Corinthians 6:3; Revelation 22:5b).

4. We will fellowship without suspicion (Matthew 8:11).

5. We will learn without weariness (1 Corinthians 13:12).

6. We will rest without boredom (Revelation 14:10-13).

9. Will We See God in Heaven?

Most of the modern heavenly memoirs contain some recollection of seeing God or at least some manifestation of his glory. Others recount seeing Jesus. What does the Bible say about seeing God and Jesus in heaven?

The Bible is clear that we will see Jesus in heaven. Jesus is the second person of the triune Godhead, who took on sinless humanity and came to live on earth. Jesus will forever be the God-man, and we will see him in heaven. First John 3:2 says, "Dear friends, we are already God's children, but he has not yet shown us what we will be like when Christ appears. But we do know that we will be like him, for we will see him as he really is." In Revelation 5, the Lamb, Jesus, is at the center of everything that's happening in heaven.

Two key passages confirm that we will also see the manifestation of God the Father in heaven. Matthew 5:8 says, "God blesses those whose hearts are pure, for they will see God." Revelation 4:2-3 strengthens the point: "Instantly I was in the Spirit, and I saw a throne in heaven and someone sitting on it. The one sitting on the throne was as brilliant as gemstones—like jasper and carnelian. And the glow of an emerald circled his throne like a rainbow." The one who sits on the throne (the throne-sitter) in Revelation 4–5 is God the Father. In Revelation 5:13 the one who sits on the throne is clearly distinguished from the Lamb (Jesus). I believe the Bible is clear that we will see God the Father in heaven. John MacArthur supports this view:

> I believe that in heaven we will see God Himself with our physical eyes. . . . God will reveal the light of His glory, and through perfect eyes we will see the very face of God. God is spirit (John 4:24), and spirit is invisible; therefore, whenever God manifests Himself He does so in the form of light. . . . Seeing Christ and the Father will eternally awe us.[11]

The distinction between seeing the Father and the Son in heaven does not mean there are many gods. The true God is Trinitarian (see Genesis 1:26; 11:7; Mark 1:10-11; 2 Corinthians 13:14). God is one (see Deuteronomy 6:4). The nature of God is often stated like this: God is one in essence or nature, yet three in person. Another way to put it is that God is one "what" (one essence) and three "whos" (three persons—Father, Son and Holy Spirit). While this truth is beyond our ability to fully grasp here on earth, we can be sure we will see the glorious manifestation of the Father in heaven as well as the face of our Lord Jesus Christ: "They will see his face, and his name will be written on their foreheads. And there will be no night there—no need for lamps or sun—for the Lord God will shine on them. And they will reign forever and ever" (Revelation 22:4-5).

10. What Kind of Body Will We Have in Heaven?

The Bible is clear that our present bodies will be resurrected just as Jesus was resurrected from the dead. Every believer in Christ will have a glorified, immortal, imperishable body that is fit for heaven. Second Corinthians 5:1-4 tells us we will have a new body:

> We know that when this earthly tent we live in is taken down (that is, when we die and leave this earthly body), we will have a house in heaven, an eternal body made for us by God himself and not by human hands. We grow weary in our present bodies, and we long to put on our heavenly bodies like new clothing. For we will put on heavenly bodies; we will not be spirits without bodies. While we live in these earthly bodies, we groan and sigh, but it's not that we want to die and get rid of these bodies that clothe

us. Rather, we want to put on our new bodies so that these dying bodies will be swallowed up by life.

Yet when we begin to think about our future bodies, we often have more questions than answers. Our present existence is all we know, and it's hard to fathom what a new body will be like. Although the Bible doesn't satisfy our curiosity about every detail of our new bodies, it does give us a basic idea of what they will be like.

First of all, we know that our new bodies will be like the resurrected, glorified body of Jesus. Philippians 3:20-21 says, "We are citizens of heaven, where the Lord Jesus Christ lives. And we are eagerly waiting for him to return as our Savior. He will take our weak mortal bodies and change them into glorious bodies like his own, using the same power with which he will bring everything under his control." First John 3:2 carries the same idea: "Dear friends, we are already God's children, but he has not yet shown us what we will be like when Christ appears. But we do know that we will be like him, for we will see him as he really is."

Since our new bodies will be like the resurrected body of Jesus, we can look at Jesus after his resurrection to learn about our future. In his resurrection body Jesus ate food. He was recognized by his disciples. He was not limited by time or space. Two different times, Jesus came right through the walls of the room where the disciples were meeting (see John 20:19, 26). Since our future bodies will be just like the resurrection body of Jesus, evidently we will be able to do the same things.

Joni Eareckson Tada, who suffered a tragic diving accident as a teenager and became a quadriplegic, can't wait to get her new body like the body of Jesus:

> Somewhere in my broken, paralyzed body is the
> seed of what I shall become. The paralysis makes
> what I am to become all the more grand when you
> contrast atrophied, useless legs against splenderous
> resurrected legs. I'm convinced if there are mirrors
> in heaven (and why not?), the image I'll see will
> be unmistakably "Joni," although a much better,
> brighter "Joni." So much so, that it's not worth
> comparing. . . . I will bear the likeness of Jesus, the
> man from heaven.[12]

The most detailed passage about our future bodies is
1 Corinthians 15:35-44, 48-49:

> Someone may ask, "How will the dead be raised?
> What kind of bodies will they have?" What a foolish
> question! When you put a seed into the ground, it
> doesn't grow into a plant unless it dies first. And
> what you put in the ground is not the plant that will
> grow, but only a bare seed of wheat or whatever you
> are planting. Then God gives it the new body he
> wants it to have. A different plant grows from each
> kind of seed. Similarly there are different kinds of

flesh—one kind for humans, another for animals, another for birds, and another for fish.

There are also bodies in the heavens and bodies on the earth. The glory of the heavenly bodies is different from the glory of the earthly bodies. The sun has one kind of glory, while the moon and stars each have another kind. And even the stars differ from each other in their glory.

It is the same way with the resurrection of the dead. Our earthly bodies are planted in the ground when we die, but they will be raised to live forever. Our bodies are buried in brokenness, but they will be raised in glory. They are buried in weakness, but they will be raised in strength. They are buried as natural human bodies, but they will be raised as spiritual bodies. For just as there are natural bodies, there are also spiritual bodies. . . . Earthly people are like the earthly man, and heavenly people are like the heavenly man. Just as we are now like the earthly man, we will someday be like the heavenly man.

These verses reveal at least six wonderful truths about our new bodies:

1. Immortal—not subject to disease, decay, or death— they will never wear out.
2. Heavenly—perfectly fitted for heaven.
3. Diverse—unique and diverse from one another just

as different stars and planets are unique and have varying degrees of glory.

4. Glorious—will never disappoint us.
5. Powerful/strong—will never get tired or weak and will never wear out or fall prey to sin.
6. Spiritual—fitted for heaven, allowing us to fully express our spiritual nature.

One final point about our new bodies is that they will have continuity with our present bodies yet vast change. Think about the resurrection body of Jesus. It looked similar to his old body. He was recognizable to his disciples, but it was also vastly, infinitely different. To reinforce this point, 1 Corinthians 15 employs the image of planting a seed as representing the placing of a body in the ground at death. A seed planted in the ground maintains continuity with the plant or tree it produces. For instance, a pumpkin seed produces a pumpkin. Grass seed becomes grass. A grain of wheat produces wheat. In all these examples there is rigid continuity between seed and plant, but there is also radical change. A tiny acorn grows into a mighty oak tree. A corn seed becomes a stately stalk. An ugly bulb comes forth as a beautiful, fragrant tulip. You can't imagine the grandeur and majesty of a majestic redwood by looking at a tiny seed. The same is true of our new body. There is continuity between the body that is buried in the ground at death but also stunning change that we can't imagine here on earth by looking at our earthly bodies.

My favorite fact about our new bodies is recorded in 1 Corinthians 15:43: "Our bodies are buried in brokenness, but they will be raised in glory. They are buried in weakness, but they will be raised in strength." Our worn-out, broken, weak bodies are laid in the grave. The bodies that rise are glorious and strong. If there's some part of your body you don't like or would change if you could, which is probably true of all of us, you can rest assured that it will be perfect on your new body. In heaven we won't need exercise classes, StairMasters, treadmills, weight rooms, cholesterol medication, Botox injections, liposuction, sugar-free food, low-calorie smoothies, vitamins, plastic surgery, or foods high in fiber. Our gracious heavenly Father will craft a glorious, unique, diverse, perfect new body for each one of his children that will never grow weary or disappoint us.

Appendix 2: Recommended Books on Heaven and the Afterlife

Alcorn, Randy. *Heaven*. Carol Stream, IL: Tyndale House, 2004.

Boa, Kenneth D. and Robert M. Bowman Jr. *Sense & Nonsense about Heaven and Hell*. Grand Rapids, MI: Zondervan, 2007.

Dixon, Larry. *Heaven: Thinking Now about Forever*. Camp Hill, PA: Christian Publications, 2002.

Ellsworth, Roger. *What the Bible Teaches about Heaven*. Webster, NY: Evangelical Press, 2007.

Enns, Paul. *Heaven Revealed*. Chicago: Moody, 2011.

Graham, Billy. *The Heaven Answer Book*. Nashville: Thomas Nelson, 2012.

Hitchcock, Mark. *55 Answers to Questions about Life After Death*. Colorado Springs: Multnomah, 2005.

Jacoby, Douglas A. *What's the Truth about Heaven and Hell?: Sorting Out the Confusion about the Afterlife*. Eugene, OR: Harvest House, 2013.

MacArthur, John. *The Glory of Heaven: The Truth about Heaven, Angels, and Eternal Life*. Wheaton, IL: Crossway, 2013.

Motyer, Alec. *Life 2: The Sequel*. Reprint, Great Britain: Christian Focus Publications, 2008.

Rhodes, Ron. *The Undiscovered Country: Exploring the Wonder of the Afterlife*. Eugene, OR: Harvest House, 1996.

Rhodes, Ron. *What Happens After Life?: 21 Amazing Revelations about Heaven and Hell*. Eugene, OR: Harvest House, 2014.

Tada, Joni Eareckson. *Heaven: Your Real Home*. Minneapolis, MN: Grason, 1995.

Appendix 3:
Scripture Passages about Heaven

Isaiah 6:1-8

It was in the year King Uzziah died that I saw the Lord. He was sitting on a lofty throne, and the train of his robe filled the Temple. Attending him were mighty seraphim, each having six wings. With two wings they covered their faces, with two they covered their feet, and with two they flew. They were calling out to each other,

> *"Holy, holy, holy is the LORD of Heaven's Armies!*
> *The whole earth is filled with his glory!"*

Their voices shook the Temple to its foundations, and the entire building was filled with smoke.

Then I said, "It's all over! I am doomed, for I am a sinful man. I have filthy lips, and I live among a people with filthy lips. Yet I have seen the King, the LORD of Heaven's Armies."

Then one of the seraphim flew to me with a burning coal he had taken from the altar with a pair of tongs. He touched my lips with it and said, "See, this coal has touched your lips. Now your guilt is removed, and your sins are forgiven."

Then I heard the Lord asking, "Whom should I send as a messenger to this people? Who will go for us?"

I said, "Here I am. Send me."

Ezekiel 1

On July 31 of my thirtieth year, while I was with the Judean exiles beside the Kebar River in Babylon, the heavens were opened and I saw visions of God. This happened during the fifth year of King Jehoiachin's captivity. (The LORD gave this message to Ezekiel son of Buzi, a priest, beside the Kebar River in the land of the Babylonians, and he felt the hand of the LORD take hold of him.)

As I looked, I saw a great storm coming from the north, driving before it a huge cloud that flashed with lightning and shone with brilliant light. There was fire inside the cloud, and in the middle of the fire glowed something like gleaming amber. From the center of the cloud came four living beings that looked human, except that each had four faces and four wings. Their legs were straight, and their feet had hooves like those of a calf and shone like burnished bronze. Under each of their four wings I could see human hands. So each of the four beings had four faces and four wings. The wings of each living being touched the wings of the beings beside it. Each one moved straight forward in any direction without turning around.

Each had a human face in the front, the face of a lion on the right side, the face of an ox on the left side, and the face of an eagle at the back. Each had two pairs of outstretched wings—one pair stretched out to touch the wings of the living beings on either side of it, and the other pair covered its body. They went in whatever direction the spirit chose, and they moved straight forward in any direction without turning around.

The living beings looked like bright coals of fire or brilliant torches, and lightning seemed to flash back and forth among them. And the living beings darted to and fro like flashes of lightning.

As I looked at these beings, I saw four wheels touching the ground beside them, one wheel belonging to each. The wheels sparkled as if made of beryl. All four wheels looked alike and were made the same; each wheel had a second wheel turning crosswise within it. The beings could move in any of the four directions they faced, without turning as they moved. The rims of the four wheels were tall and frightening, and they were covered with eyes all around.

When the living beings moved, the wheels moved with them. When they flew upward, the wheels went up, too. The spirit of the living beings was in the wheels. So wherever the spirit went, the wheels and the living beings also went. When the beings moved, the wheels moved. When the beings stopped, the wheels stopped. When the beings flew upward, the wheels rose up, for the spirit of the living beings was in the wheels.

Spread out above them was a surface like the sky, glittering like crystal. Beneath this surface the wings of each living being stretched out to touch the others' wings, and each had two wings covering its body. As they flew, their wings sounded to me like waves crashing against the shore or like the voice of the Almighty or like the shouting of a mighty army. When they stopped, they let down their wings. As they stood with wings lowered, a voice spoke from beyond the crystal surface above them.

Above this surface was something that looked like a throne made of blue lapis lazuli. And on this throne high above was a figure whose appearance resembled a man. From what appeared to be his waist up, he looked like gleaming amber, flickering like a fire. And from his waist down, he looked like a burning flame, shining with splendor. All around him was a glowing halo, like a rainbow shining in the clouds on a rainy day. This is what the glory of the LORD looked like to me. When I saw it, I fell face down on the ground, and I heard someone's voice speaking to me.

Revelation 4–5

Then as I looked, I saw a door standing open in heaven, and the same voice I had heard before spoke to me like a trumpet blast. The voice said, "Come up here, and I will show you what must happen after this." And instantly I was in the Spirit, and I saw a throne in heaven and someone sitting on it. The one sitting on the throne was as brilliant as gemstones—like jasper and carnelian. And the glow of an emerald circled his throne like a rainbow. Twenty-four thrones surrounded him, and twenty-four elders sat on them. They were all clothed in white and had gold crowns on their heads. From the throne came flashes of lightning and the rumble of thunder. And in front of the throne were seven torches with burning flames. This is the sevenfold Spirit of God. In front of the throne was a shiny sea of glass, sparkling like crystal.

In the center and around the throne were four living beings, each covered with eyes, front and back. The first of these living beings was like a lion; the second was like an ox; the third had a human face; and the fourth was like an eagle in flight. Each of these living beings had six wings, and their wings were covered all over with eyes, inside and out. Day after day and night after night they keep on saying,

> *"Holy, holy, holy is the Lord God, the Almighty—*
> *the one who always was, who is, and who is still to*
> *come."*

Whenever the living beings give glory and honor and thanks to the one sitting on the throne (the one who lives forever and ever), the twenty-four elders fall down and worship the one sitting on the throne (the one who lives forever and ever). And they lay their crowns before the throne and say,

> *"You are worthy, O Lord our God,*
> *to receive glory and honor and power.*

For you created all things,
and they exist because you created what you pleased."

Then I saw a scroll in the right hand of the one who was sitting on the throne. There was writing on the inside and the outside of the scroll, and it was sealed with seven seals. And I saw a strong angel, who shouted with a loud voice: "Who is worthy to break the seals on this scroll and open it?" But no one in heaven or on earth or under the earth was able to open the scroll and read it.

Then I began to weep bitterly because no one was found worthy to open the scroll and read it. But one of the twenty-four elders said to me, "Stop weeping! Look, the Lion of the tribe of Judah, the heir to David's throne, has won the victory. He is worthy to open the scroll and its seven seals."

Then I saw a Lamb that looked as if it had been slaughtered, but it was now standing between the throne and the four living beings and among the twenty-four elders. He had seven horns and seven eyes, which represent the seven-fold Spirit of God that is sent out into every part of the earth. He stepped forward and took the scroll from the right hand of the one sitting on the throne. And when he took the scroll, the four living beings and the twenty-four elders fell down before the Lamb. Each one had a harp, and they held gold bowls filled with incense, which are the prayers of God's people. And they sang a new song with these words:

"You are worthy to take the scroll
  and break its seals and open it.
For you were slaughtered, and your blood has ransomed
    people for God
  from every tribe and language and people and nation.
And you have caused them to become
  a Kingdom of priests for our God.
  And they will reign on the earth."

Then I looked again, and I heard the voices of thousands and millions of angels around the throne and of the living beings and the elders. And they sang in a mighty chorus:

"Worthy is the Lamb who was slaughtered—
    to receive power and riches
and wisdom and strength
    and honor and glory and blessing."

And then I heard every creature in heaven and on earth and under the earth and in the sea. They sang:

"Blessing and honor and glory and power
  belong to the one sitting on the throne
  and to the Lamb forever and ever."

And the four living beings said, "Amen!" And the twenty-four elders fell down and worshiped the Lamb.

Revelation 21–22

Then I saw a new heaven and a new earth, for the old heaven and the old earth had disappeared. And the sea was also gone. And I saw the holy city, the new Jerusalem, coming down from God out of heaven like a bride beautifully dressed for her husband.

I heard a loud shout from the throne, saying, "Look, God's home is now among his people! He will live with them, and they will be his people. God himself will be with them. He will wipe every tear from their eyes, and there will be no more death or sorrow or crying or pain. All these things are gone forever."

And the one sitting on the throne said, "Look, I am making everything new!" And then he said to me, "Write this down, for what I tell you is trustworthy and true." And he also said, "It is finished! I am the Alpha and the Omega—the Beginning and the End. To all who are thirsty I will give freely from the springs of the water of life. All who are victorious will inherit all these blessings, and I will be their God, and they will be my children.

"But cowards, unbelievers, the corrupt, murderers, the immoral, those who practice witchcraft, idol worshipers, and all liars—their fate is in the fiery lake of burning sulfur. This is the second death."

Then one of the seven angels who held the seven bowls containing the seven last plagues came and said to me, "Come with me! I will show you the bride, the wife of the Lamb."

So he took me in the Spirit to a great, high mountain, and he showed me the holy city, Jerusalem, descending out of heaven from God. It shone with the glory of God and sparkled like a precious stone—like jasper as clear as crystal. The city wall was broad and high, with twelve gates guarded by twelve angels. And the names of the twelve tribes of Israel were written on the gates. There were three gates on each side—east, north, south, and west. The wall of the city had twelve foundation stones, and on them were written the names of the twelve apostles of the Lamb.

The angel who talked to me held in his hand a gold measuring stick to measure the city, its gates, and its wall. When he measured it, he found it was a square, as wide as it was long. In fact, its length and width and height were each 1,400 miles. Then he measured the walls and found them to be 216 feet thick (according to the human standard used by the angel).

The wall was made of jasper, and the city was pure gold, as clear as glass. The wall of the city was built on foundation stones inlaid with twelve precious stones: the first was jasper, the second sapphire, the third agate, the fourth emerald, the fifth onyx, the sixth carnelian, the seventh chrysolite, the eighth beryl, the ninth topaz, the tenth chrysoprase, the eleventh jacinth, the twelfth amethyst.

The twelve gates were made of pearls—each gate from a single pearl! And the main street was pure gold, as clear as glass.

I saw no temple in the city, for the Lord God Almighty

and the Lamb are its temple. And the city has no need of sun or moon, for the glory of God illuminates the city, and the Lamb is its light. The nations will walk in its light, and the kings of the world will enter the city in all their glory. Its gates will never be closed at the end of day because there is no night there. And all the nations will bring their glory and honor into the city. Nothing evil will be allowed to enter, nor anyone who practices shameful idolatry and dishonesty— but only those whose names are written in the Lamb's Book of Life.

Then the angel showed me a river with the water of life, clear as crystal, flowing from the throne of God and of the Lamb. It flowed down the center of the main street. On each side of the river grew a tree of life, bearing twelve crops of fruit, with a fresh crop each month. The leaves were used for medicine to heal the nations.

No longer will there be a curse upon anything. For the throne of God and of the Lamb will be there, and his servants will worship him. And they will see his face, and his name will be written on their foreheads. And there will be no night there—no need for lamps or sun—for the Lord God will shine on them. And they will reign forever and ever.

Then the angel said to me, "Everything you have heard and seen is trustworthy and true. The Lord God, who inspires his prophets, has sent his angel to tell his servants what will happen soon."

"Look, I am coming soon! Blessed are those who obey the words of prophecy written in this book."

I, John, am the one who heard and saw all these things. And when I heard and saw them, I fell down to worship at the feet of the angel who showed them to me. But he said, "No, don't worship me. I am a servant of God, just like you and your brothers the prophets, as well as all who obey what is written in this book. Worship only God!"

Then he instructed me, "Do not seal up the prophetic words in this book, for the time is near. Let the one who is doing harm continue to do harm; let the one who is vile continue to be vile; let the one who is righteous continue to live righteously; let the one who is holy continue to be holy."

"Look, I am coming soon, bringing my reward with me to repay all people according to their deeds. I am the Alpha and the Omega, the First and the Last, the Beginning and the End."

Blessed are those who wash their robes. They will be permitted to enter through the gates of the city and eat the fruit from the tree of life. Outside the city are the dogs—the sorcerers, the sexually immoral, the murderers, the idol worshipers, and all who love to live a lie.

"I, Jesus, have sent my angel to give you this message for the churches. I am both the source of David and the heir to his throne. I am the bright morning star."

The Spirit and the bride say, "Come." Let anyone who hears this say, "Come." Let anyone who is thirsty come. Let anyone who desires drink freely from the water of life. And I solemnly declare to everyone who hears the words of prophecy written in this book: If anyone adds anything to what is written here, God will add to that person the plagues described in this book. And if anyone removes any of the words from this book of prophecy, God will remove that person's share in the tree of life and in the holy city that are described in this book.

He who is the faithful witness to all these things says, "Yes, I am coming soon!"

Amen! Come, Lord Jesus!

May the grace of the Lord Jesus be with God's holy people.

Notes

CHAPTER 1: HEAVEN CAN'T WAIT

1. Douglas A. Jacoby, *What's the Truth about Heaven and Hell?* (Eugene, OR: Harvest House, 2013), 11–12.
2. C. S. Lewis, "The Weight of Glory" (sermon, Church of St. Mary the Virgin, Oxford, England, June 8, 1942), http://www.verber.com/mark/xian/weight-of-glory.pdf.
3. Tal Brooke, foreword to *Heaven Can't Wait: A Survey of Alleged Trips to the Other Side* by William M. Alnor (Grand Rapids, MI: Baker Books, 1996), 9.
4. "Heaven Is for Real," *Box Office Mojo,* http://www.boxofficemojo.com/movies/?id=heavenisforreal.htm.
5. Craig Wilson, "Publishers Are in Seventh Heaven with Near-Death Memoirs," Religion News Service, January 24, 2013, http://www.religionnews.com/2013/01/24/publishers-are-in-seventh-heaven-with-near-death-memoirs/.
6. Douglas R. Groothuis, *Deceived by the Light* (Eugene, OR: Wipf and Stock Publishers, 1995), 12.
7. Jacoby, *What's the Truth about Heaven and Hell?*, 183.

CHAPTER 2: THE ABCs OF NDEs

1. Randy Alcorn, *The Law of Rewards* (Carol Stream, IL: Tyndale House, 2003), 51.
2. Courtney Coren, "Harris Poll: Belief in God Falls," *Newsmax,* December 23, 2013, http://www.newsmax.com/US/harris-poll-religion-god/2013/12/23/id/543450.
3. Michael Schroter-Kunhardt, "A Review of Near Death Experiences," *Journal of Scientific Exploration* 7, no. 3 (1993): 219–39, http://www.scientificexploration.org/journal/jse_07_3_schroter-kunhardt.pdf.

4. Eben Alexander, *Proof of Heaven: A Neurosurgeon's Journey into the Afterlife* (New York: Simon & Schuster, 2012), 133–34.

5. Alnor, *Heaven Can't Wait*, 31.

6. Gary R. Habermas and J. P. Moreland, *Immortality: The Other Side of Death* (Nashville: Thomas Nelson, 1992), 73.

7. John Ankerberg and John Weldon, *The Facts on Life After Death* (Eugene, OR: Harvest House, 1992), 7–8. See also Eben Alexander, *Proof of Heaven: A Neurosurgeon's Journey into the Afterlife* (New York: Simon & Schuster, 2012), 131.

8. Alnor, *Heaven Can't Wait*, 90–93. These elements are presented by Kenneth Ring, *Life at Death: A Scientific Investigation of the Near-Death Experience* (New York: Quill, 1982), 23–24.

9. Ankerberg and Weldon, *The Facts on Life After Death*, 8. For refutation of NDEs as the result of only natural causes, see Habermas and Moreland, *Immortality*, 92–105. Kenneth Ring discusses these various interpretations at length (*Life at Death*, 206–17).

10. Habermas and Moreland, *Immortality*, 105.

11. Ibid., 93.

12. Ibid.

13. Ibid.

14. Dinesh D'Souza, *Life After Death: The Evidence* (Washington, DC: Regnery, 2009), 72.

15. See Rodney Clapp, "Rumors of Heaven," *Christianity Today*, October 7, 1988, 20.

16. Groothuis, *Deceived by the Light*, 69.

CHAPTER 3: "I THOUGHT I'D DIED AND GONE TO HEAVEN"

1. Betty J. Eadie, *Embraced by the Light* (Carson City, NV: Gold Leaf Press, 1992), 29.

2. Ibid., 85.

3. Alnor, *Heaven Can't Wait*, 90–93. Alnor provides troubling quotes from dialogue between Eadie and interviewers on *20/20* and also Oprah Winfrey (60–63).

4. Groothuis, *Deceived by the Light*. The book contains an excellent section questioning Eadie's story about her actual physical condition at the time of her NDE and purported trip to heaven (118–21).

5. Eadie, *Embraced by the Light*, 45.

6. Ibid., 45–46.

7. Ibid., 31–32.

8. Ibid., 47–49, 52.

9. Groothuis, *Deceived by the Light*, 26.

10. Quoted in Alnor, *Heaven Can't Wait*, 18.

11. Eadie, *Embraced by the Light*, 84–85.

12. Phil Ryken, *Kingdom, Come!* (Wheaton, IL: Crossway, 2013), 79–80.

13. Ibid., 84.

14. Eadie, *Embraced by the Light*, 49.

15. Ibid., 95.

16. Ibid., 83.

17. John MacArthur, *The Glory of Heaven: The Truth about Heaven, Angels, and Eternal Life* (Wheaton, IL: Crossway, 2013), 178.

18. Mary K. Baxter, *A Divine Revelation of Hell* (New Kensington, PA: Whitaker House, 1993), 205.

19. Larry Dixon, *Heaven: Thinking Now about Forever* (Camp Hill, PA: Christian Publications, 2002), 66.

20. Mary K. Baxter, *A Divine Revelation of Heaven* (New Kensington, PA: Whitaker House, 1998), 9.

21. Baxter, *A Divine Revelation of Hell*, 61–62.

22. Baxter, *A Divine Revelation of Heaven*, 144.

23. Ibid., 54, 56.

24. Ibid., 173.

25. Ibid., 87, 90–91.

26. Ibid., 162.

27. Dixon, *Heaven*, 59.

28. Baxter, *A Divine Revelation of Hell*, 205–6.

29. Dixon, *Heaven*, 60.

30. Don Piper, *90 Minutes in Heaven* (Grand Rapids, MI: Revell, 2004), 25.

31. Ibid., 32.

32. Ibid., 33.

33. Ibid., 35.

CHAPTER 4: YOUR BEST AFTERLIFE NOW

1. Crystal McVea, *Waking Up in Heaven: A True Story of Brokenness, Heaven, and Life Again* (New York: Howard Books, 2013), 174–75.

2. Ibid., 12.

3. Ibid., 165.

4. MacArthur, *The Glory of Heaven*, 51.

5. McVea, *Waking Up in Heaven*, 164.

6. Ibid., 11.

7. Ibid., 166, 171.

8. Ibid., 198–99.

9. Ibid., 239.
10. Ibid., 199.
11. Ibid., 212–13.
12. Ibid., 233–34.
13. Kevin Malarkey and Alex Malarkey, *The Boy Who Came Back from Heaven: A Remarkable Account of Miracles, Angels, and Life beyond This World* (Carol Stream, IL: Tyndale, 2010), 31, 33.
14. Ibid., 145.
15. Ibid., 189.
16. Ibid., 188.
17. Ibid., x.
18. Ibid., 49.
19. MacArthur, *The Glory of Heaven*, 201.
20. Ibid., 201, footnote 4.
21. Malarkey, *The Boy Who Came Back from Heaven*, 170.
22. Ibid., 171.
23. Ibid., 171–72.
24. Ibid., 166–67.
25. Ibid., 167.
26. MacArthur, *The Glory of Heaven*, 208.

CHAPTER 5: DEAD WRONG

1. Mary Neal, *To Heaven and Back: A Doctor's Extraordinary Account of Her Death, Heaven, Angels, and Life Again* (Colorado Springs: WaterBrook Press, 2012), xiii.
2. Ibid., xii.
3. Ibid., 9–11.
4. Ibid., 41.
5. Ibid., 73.
6. Ibid.
7. Ibid., 147.
8. Ibid., 170.
9. MacArthur, *The Glory of Heaven*, 210.
10. Neal, *To Heaven and Back*, 98.
11. Ibid., 68–69.
12. Ibid., 103.
13. Ibid., 209.
14. Alexander, *Proof of Heaven*, 9, 78.
15. Allan J. Hamilton, endorsements for *Proof of Heaven*, i.
16. Alexander, *Proof of Heaven*, 78.

17. Ibid., 30–31.
18. Ibid., 31–32.
19. Ibid., 48, 70.
20. Ibid., 48–49.
21. Ibid., 83.
22. Ibid., 158.
23. Ibid., 161.
24. Ibid., 156.
25. Ibid., 160.
26. Ibid., 86.
27. Google search results for "Mysticism," Google.com, https://www.google.com/?gws_rd=ssl#q=mysticism.
28. Alexander, *Proof of Heaven*, 161.
29. Ibid., 157–58.
30. Ibid., 158.
31. Dr. Eben Alexander, "Proof of Heaven: A Doctor's Experience with the Afterlife," *Newsweek*, October 8, 2012, http://www.newsweek.com/proof-heaven-doctors-experience-afterlife-65327.
32. Alexander, *Proof of Heaven*, 9.
33. Ibid., 161.
34. Ibid., 48. See also pages 41, 47.
35. Ibid., 71.
36. Ibid., 148.
37. Ibid., 172.

CHAPTER 6: *HEAVEN IS FOR REAL*—IS IT FOR REAL?

1. Thomas K. Arnold, "'Heaven Is for Real' Surpasses Group of New Releases to Top Home Video Sales Chart," *Variety*, July 30, 2014, http://variety.com/2014/film/news/heaven-is-for-real-surpasses-group-of-new-releases-to-top-home-video-sales-chart-1201272545/.
2. Southern Baptist Convention, resolution, "On the Sufficiency of Scripture Regarding the Afterlife," June 10-11, 2014, http://www.sbc.net/resolutions/2247/on-the-sufficiency-of-scripture-regarding-the-afterlife.
3. Paul Mathenia, "First Person: Cuteness vs. Divine Revelation," *Baptist Press*, March 27, 2014, http://www.bpnews.net/42258.
4. Ibid.
5. Todd Burpo, *Heaven Is for Real: A Little Boy's Astounding Story of His Trip to Heaven and Back* (Nashville, TN: Thomas Nelson, 2010), 61.
6. Ibid., 76.
7. Ibid., 61.

8. Ibid.
9. Ibid., 100.
10. Tim Challies, "Heaven Is for Real," *Challies.com* (blog), March 28, 2011, http://www.challies.com/book-reviews/heaven-is-for-real.
11. Burpo, *Heaven Is for Real*, 63.
12. Ibid., 65.
13. MacArthur, *The Glory of Heaven*, 42.
14. Burpo, *Heaven Is for Real*, 67.
15. Ibid., 66.
16. D. A. Carson, *The Gospel according to John*, The Pillar New Testament Commentary (Grand Rapids, MI: William B. Eerdmans, 1991), 656.
17. Burpo, *Heaven Is for Real*, 67.
18. Ibid., 95.
19. Ibid.
20. Jacoby, *What's the Truth about Heaven and Hell?*, 181.
21. Burpo, *Heaven Is for Real*, 71–72.
22. Ibid., 101.
23. Some scholars identify the twenty-four elders in Revelation as angelic beings, and in Revelation 4:4 they are seated on thrones around God's throne. I believe the twenty-four elders are representative of the redeemed church of Jesus Christ in heaven. For a discussion of the identity of the elders, see Mark Hitchcock, *The End: A Complete Overview of Bible Prophecy and the End of Days* (Carol Stream, IL: Tyndale House, 2012), 147–48.
24. Burpo, *Heaven Is for Real*, 102–3.
25. Ibid., 105.
26. Ibid., 93.
27. Ibid., 144–45.
28. Jacoby, *What's the Truth about Heaven and Hell?*, 180.
29. Burpo, *Heaven Is for Real*, 87. Colton's mother was shocked to hear that her father (Colton's grandfather) was in heaven. She didn't believe her father would be there but learned from Colton that her father had accepted Christ twenty-eight years before his death. Yet, her father evidently never told his family members about his conversion. For one writer, this was the point that made it impossible for him to believe that Colton's story was real. He says, "Part of me wanted to believe that the boy wasn't making it all up—that his mother hadn't prompted him—but this last detail made it impossible for me to accept. Jesus taught that if we are ashamed of him, he will be ashamed of us (Mark 8:38). If we disown him, he will disown us (2 Timothy 2:12). If his grandfather became a true disciple of Christ,

how could his own family members not know? The boy's experience had become a tool for his parental sentimentality" (Jacoby, *What's the Truth about Heaven and Hell?*, 181).

30. Burpo, *Heaven Is for Real*, 89, 122.
31. Ibid., 136.
32. Randy Alcorn, *Heaven* (Carol Stream, IL: Tyndale House, 2004), 66.
33. Burpo, *Heaven Is for Real*, 136, 138.
34. Ibid., 139.
35. John Phillips, *Exploring Revelation* (Neptune, NJ: Loizeaux Brothers, 1991), 236.
36. Jacoby, *What's the Truth about Heaven and Hell?*, 181.
37. MacArthur, *The Glory of Heaven*, 47.
38. Tim Challies, "Heaven Is for Real," *Challies.com* (blog), March 28, 2011, http://www.challies.com/book-reviews/heaven-is-for-real.
39. Tim Challies, "Heaven Tourism," *Challies.com* (blog), June 18, 2012, http://www.challies.com/articles/heaven-tourism.

CHAPTER 7: TROUBLE IN PARADISE

1. An account of this story can be found in Billy Graham, *Angels: God's Secret Agents*, rev. ed. (Dallas, TX: Word Publishing, 1986), 114–15.
2. Graham, *Angels*, 116.
3. Galli, "Incredible Journeys: What to Make of Visits to Heaven," *Christianity Today*, December 21, 2012, www.christianitytoday.com/ct/2012/december/incredible-journeys.html.
4. John MacArthur, "Are Visits to Heaven for Real?" *Answers in Genesis*, March 10, 2014, https://answersingenesis.org/reviews/books/are-visits-to-heaven-for-real/.
5. MacArthur, "Are Visits to Heaven for Real?"
6. Groothuis, *Deceived by the Light*, 162.
7. A. W. Tozer, *That Incredible Christian: How Heaven's Children Live on Earth* (Reprint, Camp Hill, PA: Wing Spread, 2008), 96.
8. A. W. Tozer, *Man: the Dwelling Place of God* (Reprint, Camp Hill, PA: Wing Spread, 2008), 138.
9. Dixon, *Heaven*, 63.
10. Challies, "Heaven Tourism."
11. John Piper, "How Real Is the Book 'Heaven Is for Real'?" (podcast), March 20, 2014, https://soundcloud.com/askpastorjohn/how-real-is-the-book-heaven-is. This is episode 302 in a daily podcast titled "Ask Pastor John." In this audio clip, John Piper answers a question about the reliability of the book *Heaven Is for Real* and goes on to critique all NDE literature.

12. Ibid.
13. C. Michael Patton, "Book Review: Heaven Is for Real," *Credo House* (blog), February 6, 2011, http://www.reclaimingthemind.org/blog /2011/02/book-review-heaven-is-for-real/.
14. David Platt, *Secret Church 13*, "Heaven, Hell, and the End of the World," April 15, 2014, http://www.radical.net/blog/2014/04 /heaven-is-for-real/.
15. Alnor, *Heaven Can't Wait*, 32.

CHAPTER 8: TO HELL AND BACK

1. John Blanchard, *The Complete Gathered Gold* (Webster, NY: Evangelical Press, 2006), 295.
2. Baxter, *A Divine Revelation of Hell*, 20.
3. Ibid., 79, 81.
4. Ibid., 96.
5. Ibid., 105–7.
6. Ibid., 108–9.
7. Ibid., 185.
8. Bill Wiese, *23 Minutes in Hell* (Lake Mary, FL: Charisma House, 2006), 31.
9. Ibid., 2.
10. Ibid., 104, 107.
11. Ibid., 13.
12. Ibid., 31.
13. Baxter, *A Divine Revelation of Hell*, 111.
14. Skip Heitzig, *You Can Understand the Book of Revelation* (Eugene, OR: Harvest House, 2011), 133.
15. Donald Grey Barnhouse, *Revelation: An Expository Commentary* (Grand Rapids, MI: Zondervan, 1971), 221.
16. Baxter, *A Divine Revelation of Hell*, 129.
17. Ibid., 27.
18. Ibid., 11.
19. Wiese, *23 Minutes in Hell*, xvii–xviii.

CHAPTER 9: WHAT IS HEAVEN LIKE?

1. J. C. Ryle, "Shall We Know One Another?" in *The Quiver: An Illustrated Magazine for Sunday and General Reading*, vol. 2 (London: Cassell, Petter, and Galpin, 1867), 5.
2. Alcorn, *Heaven*, 415.
3. Terry Blankenship, "Living in the Land of the Dying" (sermon),

http://www.sermoncentral.com/sermons/living-in-the-land-of
-the-dying-terry-blankenship-sermon-on-bible-study-174094.asp.

4. J. C. Ryle, "Shall We Know One Another?", 5.

5. Paul Enns, *Heaven Revealed* (Chicago: Moody, 2011), 39.

6. Bruce K. Waltke and Cathi J. Fredricks, *Genesis: A Commentary* (Grand Rapids, MI: Zondervan, 2001), 515.

7. Bart Millard of MercyMe, "I Can Only Imagine," *Almost There* (Word, 2001), quoted in Charles R. Swindoll, *Insights on Revelation* (Grand Rapids, MI: Zondervan, 2011), 272.

8. MacArthur, *The Glory of Heaven*, 214.

9. Swindoll, *Insights on Revelation*, 273.

10. Steven J. Lawson, *Heaven Help Us!* (Colorado Springs: NavPress, 1995), 148–49.

CHAPTER 10: HOW TO BE DEAD RIGHT

1. Max Lucado, *In the Eye of the Storm* (Nashville: Thomas Nelson, 1991), 137–38.

2. Groothuis, *Deceived by the Light*, 162.

APPENDIX 1: ANSWERS TO COMMON QUESTIONS ABOUT DEATH AND HEAVEN

1. Peter Kreeft, *Everything You Ever Wanted to Know about Heaven but Never Dreamed of Asking* (San Francisco: Ignatius Press, 1990), 27.

2. Ron Rhodes, *The Undiscovered Country: Exploring the Wonder of Heaven and the Afterlife* (Eugene, OR: Harvest House, 1996), 129.

3. Arno Froese, ed., *The Midnight Call* (September 2003): 42-44.

4. Bruce K. Waltke, *Genesis* (Grand Rapids, MI: Zondervan, 2001), 63.

5. W. A. Criswell and Paige Patterson, *Heaven* (Carol Stream, IL: Tyndale, 1991), 53.

6. Kreeft, *Every Thing You Ever Wanted to Know about Heaven but Never Dreamed of Asking*, 45.

7. Ibid., 45-46.

8. Ibid.

9. Joni Eareckson Tada, *Holiness in Hidden Places* (Nashville: J. Countryman, 1999), 133.

10. These six points are taken from Thomas Ice and Timothy Demy, *The Truth about Heaven and Eternity* (Eugene, OR: Harvest House, 1997), 17–18.

11. John MacArthur, Jr., *The Glory of Heaven* (Chicago: Moody Press, 1988), 90.

12. Joni Eareckson Tada, *Heaven: Your Real Home* (Grand Rapids, MI: Zondervan, 1995), 39.

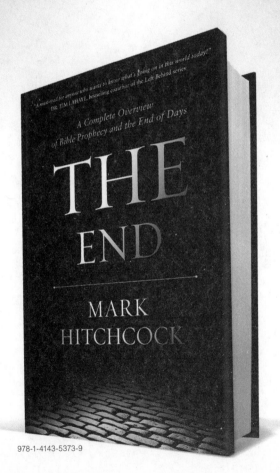